ONE WORLD
BIBLICAL PROPHECY
AND THE NEW
WORLD ORDER

ONE WORLD
BIBLICAL PROPHECY AND THE NEW WORLD ORDER

JOHN ANKERBERG
JOHN WELDON

MOODY PRESS
CHICAGO

ISBN: 0-8024-6186-7

1 2 3 4 5 6 Printing/BC/Year 95 94 93 92 91

Printed in the United States of America

About the Authors

John Ankerberg is host of the nationally televised "The John Ankerberg Show," seen each week in 39,000 American cities and also aired daily on radio. He is the founder/director of the Ankerberg Theological Research Institute. He has earned the M.A. degree in church history and the history of Christian thought, and the M.Div. degree from Trinity Evangelical Divinity School. He is currently a candidate for the doctoral degree from Bethel Theological Seminary. He is also the author and coauthor of nineteen books, including *Cultwatch*; *The Secret Teachings of The Masonic Lodge*; *When Does Life Begin? and 39 Other Tough Questions About Abortion*; *The Case for Jesus the Messiah: Incredible Prophecies That Prove God Exists*; and the Facts-On Series.

John Weldon, Ph.D., is Senior Researcher for "The John Ankerberg Show" and has studied biblical prophecy in detail. In the 1970s he was involved in the production of the most widely viewed film on biblical prophecy of all time, *The Late Great Planet Earth*. Narrated by Orson Wells and produced by Robert Amram Films of Hollywood, this film was based on the best-selling book of the decade. As one of the senior researchers for the project, Dr. Weldon conducted many months of investigation into biblical prophecy and world events. He is also coauthor with Mr. Ankerberg of a specialized text on biblical prophecy, *The Case for Jesus the Messiah: Incredible Prophecies That Prove God Exists*, and did research for Hal Lindsey on another book related to biblical prophecy, the best-selling *Hope for the Terminal Generation*. Mr. Weldon took an honors undergraduate degree in sociology at California State University, San Diego, and has a master's degree (summa cum laude) in Christian apologetics from the Simon Greenleaf School of Law in Anaheim, California. He also holds the M.Div. and D.Min. degrees from Luther Rice Seminary in Atlanta, Georgia. He also holds a third master's degree issued jointly by William Carey International University, Pasadena, California, and Pacific College of Graduate Studies, Melbourne, Australia. He earned his Ph.D. in comparative religions at Pacific College of Graduate Studies.

CONTENTS

8

PREFACE

The Gulf War and its aftermath.
The fall of Communism in Europe.
The unification of Germany.
The United States of Europe.
President Bush's new world order.
The United Nations' goal of global unity.
The Arab-Palestinian-Israeli conflict.

Suddenly the news is filled with these major events. They have all raised questions among thinking people about how these events relate to biblical prophecy. In an effort to provide the answer to such questions, we arranged a nationally televised program entitled "Current World Events and Biblical Prophecy" with two well-known authorities on the subject.

In this book we have first provided you with the transcript of that television program. Second, we have presented a fascinating interview conducted by John Ankerberg with Dave Hunt and David Breese. Third, we have presented seven key prophetic events concerning what God has said will happen in the future.

Part I
"Current World Events and Biblical Prophecy"

Introduction

Part One of this book is based on a telecast of "The John Ankerberg Show" taped before a live audience in Orlando, Florida, called "Current World Events and Biblical Prophecy." Approximately 3,000 people listened and watched as John Ankerberg interviewed guests David Breese and Dave Hunt on the connection between Bible prophecy and current world events. Both Hunt and Breese are widely published experts on end-time prophecy and current world events.

About the Television Guests

Dave Hunt is an author, researcher, and lecturer focusing on Western and Eastern religious philosophies, Christian aberrational groups and biblical prophecy. He is the author of such best-selling books on prophecy as *Peace, Prosperity and the Coming Holocaust*; *Global Peace and the Rise of Antichrist*; and novels like *The Archon Conspiracy*. His research has taken him to more than forty countries on four continents, and he is recognized internationally as an authority on cults and the occult. His writings also include biographies, novels, and devotionals. Hunt has lectured widely and is frequently interviewed on radio and television. A native of California, he graduated in 1951 from UCLA with a degree in mathematics and was licensed as a certified public accountant in 1953. He has worked as a CPA, management consultant, and general manager for numerous corporations.

David Breese, Ph.D., is an internationally-known author, lecturer, and radio broadcaster. He is president of Christian Destiny, Inc., in Hillsboro, Kansas, and is active in a ministry to college and university students, speaking to them from a background of theology and philosophy. He graduated from Judson College and Northern Seminary and has taught philosophy, apologetics, and church history. Breese travels more than 100,000 miles a year and has spoken to crowds across North America, Europe, Asia, the Caribbean, and Latin America. His lectures and debates at universities in the United States and overseas center on the confrontation between Christianity and modern thought. He is the author of several books on prophecy, including *The Mid-East Wars—Who Will Win?*; *Is Russia Off the Hook?*; *Europe and the Prince That Shall Come*; and *The Two Futures*.

1
The New World Order: Global Unity

Ankerberg: Today people want to know about biblical prophecy and the new world order that is being talked about. Also, how does the recent Gulf War fit into the biblical prophetic picture? Are the events taking place in the Middle East part of the cataclysmic world events that Jesus taught would signal His return? What specific signs did Jesus give to us that would indicate we are in the End Times—that His return to earth was near?

And immediately I must bring up the fact that some would ask, "John, don't you know this is 'prophecy'? There are so many opinions about prophecy. Or, "It's so hard to understand." Or, "It's just a minor point in the Bible, so why are you devoting so many programs to it?

But wait a minute. Is it really so minor a topic? Do you know how many verses in the Bible are devoted to prophecy? Out of the Old Testament's 23,210 verses, 6,641 verses contain prophetic information about the future. That means more than 28 percent of the entire Old Testament is concerned with prophecy. In the New Testament there are 7,914 verses, and 1,711 of them also contain predictive material. So for the entire Bible's 31,124 verses, 8,352 of them contain prophecy.

Further, twenty-three of the twenty-seven books of the New
Testament deal with the topic of the second coming of Jesus
Christ. In the New Testament alone, 318 Bible verses—every
twenty-fifth Bible verse in the New Testament—refers to the
second coming (see Part II).

Some people say, "Well, listen, I don't think it's important." Well, you have to argue with Jesus. He said to be on your
guard: "I have told you everything ahead of time. . . . When you
see these things happening, you know that it"—talking about His
return—"is near, right at the door. Be on guard! Be alert! . . .
Keep watch. . . . What I say to you, I say to everyone: 'Watch!' "
(Mark 13:23, 29, 33, 35, 37; cf. Matthew 24).

In fact, Jesus scolded the disciples for not being informed
from the Old Testament about His first coming. He said, "How
foolish you are and how slow of heart you have been not to
believe all that the prophets have spoken" (Luke 24:25). So the
"Boss" says it's important and we'd better listen.

Tonight, we're going to talk about what the Bible predicts
concerning a one-world government. George Bush is on his way
across the world promoting what he calls "the new world order."
The United Nations is talking about globalism and world unity.
So are many people today.

Dave Hunt, why do a lot of Christians see this in negative
terms, when non-Christians see emerging world unity—for
example, the coming together of the twelve European countries—as something good?

Hunt: Well, working together under a new world order will seem
like a good thing to many people because it will seem to solve
our problems. But we need to recognize something here. The war
in the Gulf was not about the price of oil at the pump—it was
about the new world order. Even Eduard Schevradnadze, speaking to the United Nations (before he resigned as foreign minister
of the Soviet Union), said, "What Saddam Hussein has done is
a threat to the new world order."

For the first time in the history of the world the United
Nations was doing what it was supposed to do. The whole world

was united against an aggressor and made a lesson out of Saddam Hussein. And it's going to make people think twice before they move in and try to take over a neighbor nation. Now, that's what the new world order is about. And one would think, "Well, it's a good thing." It can help bring peace to the world. The problem is, it leaves out the only One who can truly accomplish this, the Prince of Peace (Isaiah 9:6).

But should people uncritically accept a new world order merely because the whole world is talking about it? Hitler also had a new world order. Is the concept of a "new world order" really anything new? The first idea of a new world order began long ago. In Isaiah 14 Satan hoped to begin a "new world order" through rebellion against God. He said, "I will be like the most High," and "I will exalt my throne above the [throne] of God." So a new world order was, first of all, proposed by Satan, who was not satisfied with the universe as God made it. After his rebellion against God and his being cast out of heaven, he came down to earth and talked Adam and Eve into a new world order—into joining his rebellion (Genesis 3).

Another new world order is seen at the Tower of Babel when humanity attempted to unite against God's will. And God, displeased with what man was doing—assaulting His throne—scattered humanity and confounded their languages (Genesis 11).

What is the new world order about today? People are thinking we're going to undo what God did at Babel! We're going to get everybody back together. We're going to bring world unity. All people are going to speak the same language.

I even saw an ad placed in *Scientific American* by Lockheed promoting the idea of international cooperation through multinational corporations. They used the Tower of Babel as a symbol—and they literally said, "We are working against the Babel effect."

In Acts 17, Paul tells us why God scattered men and determined the bounds of their habitation. He said it was so that men should seek God—that they might search after Him and find Him. But people today are not seeking after God, they're seeking after their own self-interests—after false gods and the "god" within, seeking to prove so-called "human potential." Unfortunately, in seeking world peace they are ignoring the true God and relying entirely on their own powers (see Jeremiah 17:5).

Although our president, George Bush, may very well be a born-again Christian—he claims to be—unfortunately, he leaves God out of his plans for a new world order. It seems to offer more of a humanistic world order that is setting the stage for the Antichrist—a world order that will ultimately fail.

Ankerberg: Dr. David Breese, what must the new world order contain? Give me a few more thoughts about global unity and the one-world government and where the Bible says history is headed.

Breese: I concur with Dave's analysis. The President—any national leader—needs to be very careful when he states an oft-repeated suggestion of a plan. Someone once noted, "Every word the President uses weighs a ton."

The current new world order seems to be a call for something—but no one knows exactly what it's supposed to be. But obviously, if we're going to have a new world order, Middle East security requires that we be concerned with world peace. President Bush has said, "We would like to have an order in which every nation of the world has the opportunity to achieve its noblest aspirations." But the problem is that each nation's agenda is a very subjective thing.

Hussein tried this approach in the Middle East. The "new world order"—the United Nations coalition—stood against it. One interesting development of the Mid-East war was the tremendous concessions the U.S. made to the United Nations. America didn't move at all, apart from U.N. permission. This greatly strengthened the United Nations' prestige in the world.

And it occurs to me that maybe we ought to compare the ideology of our new world order with the new world order of Babel as found in the Bible. "And the whole earth was of one language and of one speech. And it came to pass, as they journeyed from the east, that they found a plain in the land of Shinar;

and they dwelt there. And they said one to another, Go to, let us make brick, and burn them thoroughly. And they had brick for stone, and slime had they for mortar. And they said, Go to, let us build us a city and a tower, whose top may reach unto heaven; and let us make us a name" (Genesis 11:1-4; KJV*).

A twofold ideology characterized this early attempt to rebel against God: one, that man can have culture without God; two, that man can build by his own efforts a tower that can take him to the heavens. In other words, this new world order offered men unity based on freedom from God: culture without God and religion without divine revelation.

For example, I think we have to understand that political internationalism is not the will of God. Nationalism is God's will. God has ordained individual nations and not a complex of nations. In Acts 17:26, we read: "And hath made of one blood all nations of men for to dwell on all the face of the earth, and hath determined the times before appointed, and the bounds of their habitation" (KJV).

It's interesting that Revelation chapters 17 and 18 give us the final *reductio ad absurdum* of such united world order. The future religious Babylon is called the great harlot who sits on the waters. This commercial Babylon is described, and it's almost as if you have a shopping list of the world's goods as you walk through a warehouse. All these things that the future united world depended on are destroyed in one hour.

During the Millennium, a world will exist in which people are united under the rulership of Jesus Christ. But when men try in their own unregenerate power to put together a complex of nations and make them cohere without God, then you have built into that complex the seeds of its own destruction. And that's exactly what will happen to this future world order that men are working on now.

---

*King James Version.

Ankerberg: Dave, the Bible identifies a future world leader called the Antichrist. You have said paradoxically that he will seem to be like Christ. Tell us how he can both deceive the world and yet appear to be a Christian.

Hunt: This new world order will be ruled by the Antichrist. In Greek, "anti" has two meanings. One of them is the meaning we always associate with "opposed to" or "against." The other meaning is "in the place of" or "a substitute for."

The Antichrist, in my opinion, will embody both meanings. He will indeed oppose Christ but in the most diabolically clever way he possibly could—anything less would not be worthy of Satan's genius. He will oppose Christ by pretending to be Christ and thus perverting Christianity from within.

Now, if indeed he pretends to be Christ, then who are his followers? They can only be those calling themselves "Christians." Paul said, "That day shall not come, except there come [an apostasy] a falling away first" (2 Thessalonians 2:3; KJV). So, I believe there has to be a new "Christianity" created that embraces all religions and, in turn, will be accepted by the other religions of the world.

Amazingly enough it is the Christianity Gorbachev talks about. It is the kind of Christianity the Pope talks about. The Pope has gone to the Muslims, the Hindus, to the Buddhists. In 1986 at Assisi he had a day of world prayer where he invited sixty of the leaders of the world's twelve major religions—even Animists and fire worshipers. The Pope made the astounding statement that "all of our prayers are creating *a spiritual energy* that is bringing forth a climate for peace."

And when the Pope went to India and spoke in Calcutta to the University of New Delhi, he said, "We haven't come here to teach you anything, we've come here to learn from your rich spiritual heritage. The world does well to pay heed to the spiritual vision of mankind that Hinduism has given to this world."

Can you imagine the apostle Paul on Mars Hill in Athens saying, "We haven't come here to teach you anything; we've come here to learn from your rich spiritual heritage?" So now we're seeing a new kind of "Christianity" being presented by the Pope and that can be embraced by all religions—and which will one day be overseen by the Antichrist himself.

Ankerberg: Dave Hunt, will the Arabs also follow an apostate religion?

Hunt: I believe so. I think that's part of what's happening in the Gulf, through the Gulf War.

Ankerberg: How?

Hunt: We've seen the Iron Curtain come down, right? Before this we had entire ministries that were anti-Communist based. The big fear was, "Communism is going to take over the world." But instead of Communism moving West, democracy is moving East. It's not going to last long, but there's an opening for the gospel right now.

So, we've talked about the Iron Curtain, but not many people talk about the Islamic curtain. I think the Islamic curtain is going to come down, too. Consider the following facts. First, Islam is not a tolerant religion. For example, today it is against the law to be a Christian in Saudi Arabia; you have to be a Muslim to be a citizen of that country. During the Gulf War, our military chaplains were even forced to remove the cross of Christ from their uniforms!

Yet the intolerance of Islam has recently received a major shock. We've had an incredible demonstration of something the world has never seen before. Muslims have watched as *infidels* have protected Muslims in spite of the fact that the Koran teaches, "Put them [intransigent non-Muslims] to death wherever you find them. . . . Kill them. . . . Over such men we give you absolute authority" (Sura [a chapter in the Koran] 4:90-93). That's what Muslims are supposed to do with infidels.

Instead of that, the Emir of Kuwait stands in front of the United Nations and appeals to a world of infidels. And what does he ask? He asks the infidels to come and restore his country from another *Islamic* leader who, in the name of *Allah*, is raping and plundering his nation. So, it took infidels to defend Mecca and

Medina, the two holiest places in the Islamic world. That's got to make Arabs think.

Also, remember that before the war Saddam himself said, "We're going to see who's on the side of God and who's on the side of Satan." Truer words were never spoken!

So I think the Islamic curtain's got to come down. Disillusionment is building. The Emir of Kuwait has got to allow democracy to come in, and I think it's going to begin a new freedom through the Islamic world that's going to open the door for the gospel, perhaps as never before.

Breese: I think that this is certainly a time to pray that out of the events of this last couple of years a tremendous Christian influence could be brought into the Muslim world. You know, it has been very difficult to reach Muslims for Christ. Many times a lifetime of effort has produced only a few converts. But now we are beginning to see Muslim converts happening in a small way. And wouldn't it be great if out of this God would open a window of opportunity to reach Muslims—even if it were only for a brief time.

Hunt: I think He will.

Breese: Perhaps millions of these people could be won for Christ. This is something for which we must pray.

2
Europe and the Antichrist

Ankerberg: David Breese, magazines such as *Time* and *Life* have all reported that twelve European nations have agreed to join together in 1992. You have written about this in your book *Europe and the Prince That Shall Come.* You have said that this group of nations will make a fantastic impact on the world and also you believe that a new political leader will emerge, the one the Bible calls "the prince that shall come." Tell us what you mean. Does the Bible speak about this and how does a coming world ruler fit in?

Breese: Well, John, that is certainly a relevant subject to our time. Why? Because a most dramatic and provocative event right now is the stated intention of Europe to become a United States of Europe—which they hope to accomplish by 1992.

So the time of European unification is now upon us. In light of this, we should notice a very interesting verse from the Old Testament. The prophet Daniel tells us,

> Know and understand this: From the issuing of the decree to restore and rebuild Jerusalem until the Anointed One, the ruler, comes, there will be seven "sevens," and sixty-two "sevens" [i.e., 483 years]. It will be rebuilt with streets and a trench, but in

times of trouble. After the sixty-two "sevens," the Anointed One will be cut off and will have nothing. The people of the ruler who will come will destroy the city and the sanctuary. The end will come like a flood: War will continue until the end, and desolations have been decreed. (Daniel 9:25-27)

Daniel says that there will be a people who will destroy the city of Jerusalem and its sanctuary, the Temple. They will also be responsible for the legal or judicial basis upon which the Messiah would be cut off—killed.

Who were the people that destroyed Jerusalem? It was the Romans. They were the ones who instituted the legal system by which Jesus Christ was crucified. Daniel implied that if we could discern who those people are, then we could watch for their reconstitution in the world because they would be the people to produce "the ruler who shall come"—who is the Antichrist.

Let's digress a moment to understand this prophecy. Daniel discusses four great empires—Neo-Babylon, Medo-Persia, Greece, and Rome. Rome was the powerful empire in the world at the time of the life of Christ. We all know that Rome fell.

But in one sense, Rome never has been dissolved—even though politically it came apart approximately A.D. 450. It never completely dissolved because it continued in the form of a religion that was a direct extension of the political power of Rome in those days.

How? Christianity arose while Rome was still in power. Later the Emperor Constantine converted to Christianity and used Christianity to solidify his empire. The empire of Rome supposedly became "Christian." So when Rome's political power dissolved, all that was left was the *religion* of Rome—which evolved into Roman Catholicism.

How does this fit into biblical prophecy? According to Daniel, the political and spiritual power of Rome will be reconstituted as a political entity at the end of the age. In other words, when we see Europe come together as it was in Roman times, then we should watch for the rise of the Antichrist.

Europe has now declared that it will be a United States of Europe by 1992. When it does, it will have 320 million people and a gross national product larger than that of the United States. In other words, it will instantly become the most powerful economic and political entity on earth. In my opinion, this uniting of Europe must follow an inevitable five-step process.

First will come economic unity. But they will soon discover, however, that you cannot have economic unity unless you quickly impose political unity, the second step.

And then third they must produce military unity. The world has learned from the tragic experience of Kuwait that if you are wealthy, you had better protect your interests. Kuwait forgot this and suffered immeasurably. A United Europe is likely to take appropriate measures to protect its great wealth.

Fourth, there will be an almost irresistible urge to find a great leader, for a leader is one who galvanizes the attention of people and consolidates power for protection of the empire. As a new entity, the United States of Europe will sense its own fragility and be open to self-protective measures. But it will also soon discover what every political power has discovered up until now, and that is, while power is relatively easy to achieve, it is difficult to sustain.

In past history, the Roman emperors took concrete, calculated actions to sustain their power. They decided that they needed not only respect and admiration, but obedience and worship. They declared themselves to be gods. In my opinion, that is the fifth and final step a United Europe will acquiesce to. It is precisely what Europe must accept if it is to produce and sustain a great leader that can hold that unparalleled conglomerate together.

Revelation 13 tells us that this is precisely the devil's plan for the future. He will put his king, the Antichrist, upon the throne. He will eventually produce a global religion and cause all the world to worship the Antichrist. The Antichrist will have power to work unheard-of miracles—miracles so stupendous they will cause the world to be stunned with admiration.

But beyond all this, he will organize the world in such a fashion that every person is required to accept some kind of a mark in the right hand or forehead. Without this special identification they cannot buy or sell.

So what does Bible prophecy suggest for our future? The Bible tells us that we can know when we are moving toward the end of the age.

There are two geopolitical things we must watch. One is that Jerusalem shall be trodden down by the Gentiles until the times of the Gentiles be fulfilled (Luke 21:24). Has that time come? Apart from the Muslim Dome of the Rock, Jerusalem is now in Jewish control. Thus, we seem to be close to fulfilling Jesus' prophecy.

The second thing to watch for is that Rome will somehow be revived. A United States of Europe comes so close to that prediction that everyone should be watching and remembering that Europe has set a date, 1992, for this to happen.

Additionally, we should watch for the emergence of a great leader out of this group of nations. We should also watch for that leader to make some very frightening announcements about his plans for the future. That is now where we are in the scheme of things.

Hunt: John, let me give one more verse to add to what Dave was saying. Some people would wonder, "How do you know that this empire will be revived?" Interestingly, *Princeton Economics* magazine said recently that in 1992 we will have Europe reconstituted 'as it was during the Holy Roman Empire.' To have a secular research group bring that kind of religious terminology into the discussion is significant.

But, how do we know this is going to happen? Because of one particular verse. I think some of the most powerful verses are in Daniel 2:41-45, which refer to the image of a man in Daniel's vision. In verse 44, Daniel refers to the ten toes of that image and says that this revised empire will emerge "in the days of these kings."

But there never were ten kings that ruled the Roman Empire. In fact, I personally think it's going to be more than just ten nations of Western Europe; I think that ultimately the whole world will be divided into ten regions. But whatever one thinks, there is a revival of the Roman Empire under ten heads (Daniel 7:24), and the Bible says very clearly "in the days of these kings shall the God of heaven set up a kingdom that will never be destroyed" (Daniel 2:44).

We also read of a stone cut "without hands" out of a mountain (i.e., supernaturally). This stone smashes the image—all the kingdoms of mankind—and after this God sets up His kingdom. So, I see the Bible predicting the reconstitution of the Roman Empire but in a worldwide form.

Ankerberg: Dave Hunt, in your book you've said somewhere at this very moment you think that on planet earth the Antichrist is almost certainly alive, biding his time, awaiting his cue. Already a mature man, he is probably active in politics, perhaps even an admired world leader whose name is almost daily on everyone's lips. One momentous day, though, Satan will utterly possess him. Now, when that happens, besides the charisma, besides the economic base, besides the military base, why will the world follow this man? Would you please talk about the supernatural aspect of it?

Hunt: In 2 Thessalonians 2:9-10, we are told this man, the Antichrist, "will come in accordance with the work of Satan displayed in all kinds of counterfeit miracles, signs and wonders, and in every sort of evil that deceives those who are perishing."

Here we see God's judgment upon an unbelieving world, one that stoops so low as to worship the Antichrist. We see a delusion imposed by God upon people who have clearly and deliberately rejected the truth. A man who comes with these incredible powers will be welcomed by all and yet will be a devil.

But how are the Buddhists and Hindus and Muslims and everybody else going to unite with this political and economic unity? I think the rapture is the key event that fits the pieces of the puzzle together.

Just think about it for a moment. If suddenly, every true Christian in the world vanishes—80 million people vanish from China, maybe 40 or 50 million from the Soviet Union, maybe 100 million from Africa, I don't know how many millions from the United States—think of what that would do to the world. Suddenly you are left behind. You have literally seen people vanish in mid-sentence—poof—they're gone! It could possibly make you insane. You have seen happen what was previously unimaginable.

The rapture will be the most incredible event to ever happen in the entire history of the world. More than all the chaos it will cause, imagine the terror! A paralyzing terror could strike the heart of every person left behind! They will ask, "Where on earth did all these people go? Who, or what took them? Is some intergalactic power snatching slaves? Who might be next? Could I be next?" Here is the possibility for real, absolute terror.

And just think of it. In the midst of all this, a man arises, and he has the answer. He explains it. He soothes everyone's fears. According to him, it's not the good guys who left, it's the bad guys that were taken.

Some New Agers are talking in these terms. They say the earth is about to experience 'a quantum leap' in consciousness. Those who are spiritually unevolved—the metaphysically ignorant—will not be able to make this quantum leap to a higher state of consciousness. They will instantly be removed to a nonphysical dimension. Before they are allowed back on a physical plane, their "karma" (bad deeds) must be dealt with.

Now, that's only one explanation. UFO cultists, those who believe in extra-terrestrial intelligences (ETI) offer another. UFO sightings and encounters today are having a far more serious impact on world culture than most people realize. Even Assad, the president of Syria, is a committed believer in ETIs. These cultists believe that advanced civilizations from space are preparing to impose a new world order on the earth. Assad himself believes this. The UFO/ETI believers have been told through spiritistic revelations that everybody who is not willing to go along with the new world order will instantly be beamed aboard massive mother ships and taken off as slaves to another planet, where their minds will be reprogrammed. Only then will they be allowed to return.

So even today many people are expecting something like a mass disappearance to happen. And talk about uniting the world! If we were only the survivors of a plane crash, for example, we would have come through the greatest disaster conceivable; a special bond would exist with every survivor. When the rapture happens, everyone left on earth will have a tremendous sense of unity. They will sense a new destiny arising for planet earth, a new age dawning with a new leader who has all the power of God—or seems to. But he will really be empowered by Satan, claiming to be God. And yet he will seem to bring peace to this world. It's going to be a time of great delusion.

Breese: Let me say that when I first heard of the Antichrist coming to the Temple in Jerusalem and setting up an image of himself that can speak like a man, what the Bible calls the abomination of desolation (Matthew 24:15), I thought, *How could people ever be fooled that the image was a real person?* Then I visited EPCOT Center right here in Orlando and got an idea of what the image might be like.

Disney has created machines that look like men. They seem to carry on conversations with people. (They have a more animated personality and a larger sense of humor than some human beings I know!) This gave me a real feeling for the kind of miracle described in Revelation 13:15, where the image of the Antichrist is supernaturally brought to life.

Ankerberg: Dr. Breese, what should people do with this information if they do not know the Lord Jesus Christ? Also, what difference could this make to Christians?

Breese: One of the greatest verses on prophecy answers that question. In 2 Peter 3:11 it says, "Seeing then all these things shall be dissolved, what manner of persons ought you to be in all holy conversation and godliness?"

What manner of persons? First, every person should become a Christian. Why? So that they may be assured that his/her sins are forgiven and that they have everlasting life. God tells us these things concerning the future—so that we will build our lives on the only secure foundation available, namely, Jesus Christ. "For other foundation can no man lay than that which is laid, which is Jesus Christ" (1 Corinthians 3:11; KJV).

Second, all of us who believe the gospel should be grabbed out of our neutrality, our mediocrity, and our disinterest to become articulate and forceful witnesses for Christ.

I think all of us agree. Around the world, we are now seeing the greatest curiosity ever about what the Bible teaches concerning future events. The world is ready, it is curious, it is vulnerable. May God help us to reach it for Christ in these last days.

Ankerberg: All right. Next, we're going to talk about the nation of Israel. What does God's Word say will happen to Israel in the future? The very fact of its existence as a nation was prophesied by the Lord thousands of years ago. That has already taken place in 1948, and now certain intriguing things are starting to happen in the Middle East with regard to prophecy. We'll examine that in detail in chapter 3.

3

The Role of Israel

Ankerberg: Everywhere I have gone in the last few months—whether it's the airline stewardesses or the barber, people are asking, "How do the events that are taking place in the Middle East and around the world square with what the Bible is saying?" And that is the very subject we are talking about.

One of the most important signs that Jesus Christ said would signal his return is the nation of Israel. Israel is a prophetic sign that would indicate the prophetic time clock is moving and ticking. According to Jesus, when we see certain things happen, boy, our antennae had better go up.

Hunt: There are four amazing prophetic facts that we need to recognize concerning Israel. First, the Bible states the Jews would be scattered throughout the world under the punishment of God—yet not be wholly assimilated into the nations. They would remain an identifiable ethnic group. This has happened and is an amazing fact in itself.

Second, God predicts that the Jews would not only survive as an ethnic people, but that they will also return to the land of Palestine centuries later.

Third, after returning to Palestine, this insignificant piece of real estate will be the focus of world attention week after week.

This is exactly what the Bible prophesied: "Behold, I will make Jerusalem a cup of trembling unto all the people round about. . . . And in that day will I make Jerusalem a burdensome stone for all people: all that burden themselves with it shall be cut in pieces, though all the people of the earth be gathered together against it" (Zechariah 12:2-3; KJV).

Israeli forces would rival in power those nations surrounding them. It is incredible to realize that even though Israel holds only one-sixth of one percent of the land in the Arab world, it has been more than a match for the surrounding Arab nations, though they outnumber Israel about forty to one.

For a moment, let's think of what these prophecies are telling us about the Bible itself. The Bible is absolutely unique. It not only contains prophecy about Israel; it also contains prophecy about other things as well. This is significant because you are not going to find any predictive prophecies like we are talking about in other holy books such as the Muslim Koran or in the Hindu Vedas or in the Book of Mormon. I don't care where you look, you just won't find it. The Bible is absolutely unique.

Ankerberg: According to the Bible, God gave us biblical prophecy "so that all the people of the earth may know that the Lord is God and that there is no other" (e.g., Ezekiel 38:23). God also said in Isaiah 46:4, 10, 11: "To whom will you compare me? To whom will you liken me? I make known the end from the beginning, from ancient times, what is still to come. I say: My purpose will stand, and I will do all that I please. What I have said, that will I bring about; what I have planned, that will I do."

God challenged anybody else in any other religion to come up with information like that which is found in the Bible. The Jew and Israel are primary examples of God's giving evidence that the Bible is His Word.

Let me ask you another question, Dave. Why do we have anti-Semitism all through history? Where did it start?

Hunt: Well, first of all, it goes back to the fact that the Jews forsook their God. They went into idolatry and immorality and the paganism of the nations that they displaced after they conquered the land of Canaan. Back in Deuteronomy 28 and other places Moses had warned them that if they did not obey the voice of the Lord their God, they would be scattered throughout the whole world. They would cry out in the morning, "Would God it were evening" and at night, "Would God it were morning." They would be persecuted and hated and killed. Now all that happened. But, in spite of all that, they have retained their national identity. It's really incredible. . . . I mean, I think I'm a mixture of Scottish, Irish, Norwegian, French, you name it!

Breese: Mongolian!

Hunt: OK, a little Mongolian. But that these people, the Jews, have been scattered throughout all the world for 1,900 years since the Diaspora and 2,500 years since the Babylonian captivity—and yet remain an identifiable ethnic national entity—and now are brought back to their land, it's incredible!

But why were they hated? It goes way back to Genesis 12, where God predicted that through Abraham and his seed all the nations of the earth will be blessed. They will be blessed because from that seed God predicted the Messiah Himself would come. He would be a Jew, descended from Abraham. So if Satan could have annihilated the Jews as a race before the Messiah came, Satan would have defeated God's stated plan of redemption.

But even now, after Christ's death on the cross, if Satan could wipe out Israel, he would derail God's future promises to Israel and thus show God to be a liar.

I think it is significant that the destruction of Israel is what the Arabs would like to do—they would love to wipe out Israel. It's written right into the Constitution of the PLO—the complete annihilation of Israel.

And anti-Semitism . . . you've got to face the fact that something is unique about these Jewish people. Remember the Pogroms persecution in Russia, Hitler's Holocaust. And even today anti-Semitism is rising again, so much so that Israel is thinking of airlifting the remaining 7,000 Jews out of Poland because it is no longer safe for them. Recently spray painted on the Jewish national theater in Warsaw is "Jews to the ovens!" Incredible, isn't it? Even today, Jewish cemeteries are being desecrated around the world.

Breese: Maybe we could throw a thought in here, too. The apostle Paul says, as he describes the human race in Romans Chapter 1, that they are full of "envy, murder, debate, deceit, malignity, whisperers, backbiters, haters of God, despiteful, proud, boasters, inventors of evil things, disobedient to parents" (vv. 29-30; KJV) . . . it's a terrible list. Consider the description "haters of God." Is it possible that in the perverse mind of man the most fulfilling way to hate God is to focus on God's own chosen people—the people who gave us what we call our Judeo-Christian heritage?

Consider this: The Bible predicts that every nation of the world will one day gather against the city of Jerusalem to do battle with her, apparently hoping to wipe out that remembrance of God. Why? Because then autonomous man can have it his own way—which, of course, he never will. The moment he becomes totally autonomous, he dies. But it seems as if both the Jew in Jerusalem and our own Judeo-Christian heritage have become a physical object of hatred—an innate hatred caused by man's sinful rebellion against God.

Ankerberg: Dr. Breese, we've mentioned that prophecy predicted the Jews would return to their land and form a nation. That's happened. The Bible prophesied that they would take over the capital of Jerusalem, their holy place. That's happened. And third, Scripture tells us they will rebuild their Temple. The drawing plans are there. The utensils for use in the new temple are actually being made.

But right now George Bush is getting ready to go to the Holy Land, proposing the idea that the Jews give up land for peace. What is the Israeli strategy? Take us into the mind of a Jewish person. What would they be thinking as they see Bush and the world trying to force them to give up land so there will be peace?

Breese: Yes, we can immediately expect strong pressure for a peace conference. The initial agenda will be peace in the Middle East. But agendas change, and soon it will not just be peace in the Middle East, but world peace. For now, the focus will be upon the state of Israel. And you can be sure that there will be pressure to give up land for peace. But in my opinion, the day that Israel gives up land to the Arabs is the day that shrimps learn to whistle!

The reason is this: If the West Bank were gone, Israel would retain only a narrow stretch of land 15 or 16 miles wide, a fragile area that could be overthrown in seconds. It's ridiculous to think they will surrender the West Bank.

I'll never forget a conversation I had in the Knesset as I talked extensively with an Israeli leader. We finished discussing the military situation, and he said to me, "Dave, remember something. In the battles of the Middle East, the Arabs could lose many times over and still come back. We can only lose once and we are finished." And then he said, "To be or not to be, that is the question!" Well, if the question is your very existence, then you cannot afford those diplomatic niceties where you set up a conference and meet with someone three weeks from now and appoint a few committees and have a cocktail party and table the motion. They have got to decide *now* what to do about any threat.

Israel is the most instantly responsive military power in the world. It's possible for the Israeli chiefs of staff to meet at midnight and to have the air force flying by four o'clock in the morning.

The reason, of course, is because the question with Israel is not, "What do you do to please the world?" or, "How do you get along with so-called diplomats of the world?" The question is, "How do we *survive*?" And when you are facing a person for whom the question is *survival*, all of the other niceties may still be nice, but they don't mean a thing.

Ankerberg: Dave Hunt, what have the Arab leaders been saying about Israel? Do you think they really want peace with Israel?

Hunt: I honestly don't think so, John. Let me give you a couple of quotes that reflect their real thinking.

First of all, Yasser Arafat's uncle was the former Grand Mufti of Jerusalem and a friend of Hitler. One time while he was visiting Germany, over Radio Berlin he said to the Arabs, "Rise as one man and kill the Jews wherever you find them. This pleases God and religion—and God is with you."

Today, his nephew Arafat says, "Our struggle with Israel is such that when it is finished, Israel will cease to exist. There can be no compromise." And I can quote on and on. So anything that the Arabs say to the contrary about their peaceful intents, it's just not true.

Breese: Consider this: Israel may have occupied Arab lands, but Israel is also the only nation on the face of the earth whose borders are defined by God Himself! And the borders of Israel reach from the river Euphrates to the great river of Egypt (Genesis 15:18).

I would hate to be the general commissioned to dislodge the Jews from that area. You'd have to kill every one of them twice! What we are asking them to do is not only ridiculous from a military and security viewpoint, it's also ridiculous in the face of a divine mandate.

Hunt: There is another problem—you've got to understand Islam to understand the nature of the situation in the Middle East. The Koran *claims* to accept the Bible, but in fact it contradicts it. For example, it denies that Jesus died for our sins.

Breese: That's true.

Hunt: According to the Koran, somebody else died in Jesus' place instead. But more apropos to our subject, the Koran teaches that it was not *Isaac* who was offered upon the altar and to whom the land was promised, (i.e., Isaac's descendants, the Jews), but it was *Ishmael* who was offered by Abraham upon the altar. Therefore, according to Islam, it was the descendants of Ishmael, *the Arabs*, who were promised this land.

Moreover, if the Jews now exist in the land promised them by God, that undermines the very foundation of Islam. No one can underestimate the importance of this fact. The Muslims must destroy Israel or they must admit that Allah is not the true God and that the Koran does not tell the truth. For every Muslim, the very existence of Israel is a powerful threat to his concept of God, his religion, and the beliefs he holds most dear.

Ankerberg: Dr. Breese, what's the importance of this topic we've been talking about?

Breese: The Bible says that at this present time the Jews who were the natural branches were taken out in order that the unnatural branches, namely all of us, should be included in God's great program of grace. And then it says that if that became salvation to us, "what shall the receiving of them be but life from the dead?" (Romans 11:15; KJV). What a beautiful day is coming!

But in the meantime I hope that every one of us will see the wisdom of knowing Jesus Christ as personal Savior, which puts us in the divine plan that reaches from here to eternity. No one needs to feel left out, because Jesus said that "whosoever will, let him [come]" (Revelation 22:17). And that goes for everyone, Jew and Gentile alike, in this amazing hour of grace. That's my recommendation.

Ankerberg: We're going to continue looking at world events and biblical prophecy. A lot of people say that there's only one superpower left right now and that's the United States, and Russia is a second-class power. Is Russia really no longer a threat? What does the Bible predict about Russia? What part will it play in events in the Middle East in the days ahead? That is what we are going to look at next.

4
The Role of the Soviet Union

Ankerberg: All of us are acquainted with the fact that some major historical events have taken place in Europe. For example, all across Europe, Communism has collapsed. But how does the collapse of Communism in the Eastern Bloc countries, and even Russia, fit into the biblical prophetic picture?

Right now, some are describing Russia as a second-class power. After the Gulf War, in which the United States stretched its muscles, if you will, and showed the world the fantastic military technology we have, many consider us to be the Number One superpower in the world.

In comparison, in Russia, the economy is bad. They can't get their economic system to work in any shape or form. Even President Gorbachev seems to be hanging by a thread. This causes many people to conclude that Russia is really no longer a threat to the world.

What does the Bible have to say concerning Russia in the days ahead?

Dr. David Breese, you've written a book entitled *Is Russia Off the Hook?*, which actually comes out of a biblical verse (Ezekiel 38:4). And I would like you to explain what that verse is and what the Bible says, and how you analyze the Soviet Union.

Breese: Well, John, as we think about the Soviet Union, it is becoming popular to say that it's all falling apart, that Communism has failed and all the rest. The implied promise of the U.S.S.R. is that they are no longer interested in world conquest. We're now thinking that peace will naturally result from the changes in the U.S.S.R.

But at this point we should be more cautious than ever. When one is dealing with a dictatorship, one should never believe what is *said* about peace and safety; instead one should always look at their *capabilities*. For example, the Soviets have said that promises are like pie crusts—made to be broken. The Soviets have demonstrated that they are masters of deceit. Because they have not yet demonstrated their ability to be trusted, the only thing that matters is their history of deception and their capability.

Colin Powell, chairman of the Joint Chiefs of Staff, and in my opinion a very heroic man, made the following point: "You know we have been looking at the Middle East, but let's not forget that there is only one nation in the world that can destroy us in 30 minutes: the Soviet Union." This is coming from our leading military officer, and we should heed his words.

What is the outcome of the Soviet Union according to Scripture? Perhaps we can first expect the arising of a grand program promising the world that things have changed, that Communism has failed, and therefore, that this former aggressor has become a benign power. But biblically, that will not be the case; Russia will retain her military might.

The Scripture says in Ezekiel 38 that God will put hooks into the jaws of the Russian army and bring it into battle. The Bible is very clear: "I will turn thee back and put hooks into thy jaws, and I will bring thee forth, all thine army, horses, and horsemen, all of them clothed with all sorts of armor, even a great company with bucklers and shields, all of them handling swords" (Ezekiel 38:4; KJV). In brief, the Scriptures predict in Ezekiel 38 that the prince of Rosh, Meshech, and Tubal will move to the south in an attempt to conquer the nation of Israel.

According to many respected Bible scholars, the prince of Rosh is Russia.

Further, Russia will move an army to the south, and that army will assault the nation of Israel in its northern mountains. And incredibly the Scripture says that five-sixths of that army will be destroyed and one-sixth will be hurled back in defeat and disgrace.

Out of that destruction, Russia's attempted conquest of Israel, will come the tremendous principle that God mentions so often in the Old Testament: "They [all the nations] shall know that I am the Lord."

I would say one other thing about the Soviet Union, and that is this. Remember that the Soviet Union is the only nation in the world that has atheism officially written into its constitution. They actively promote the idea that there is no God. But the Bible teaches, "The fool has said in his heart, 'There is no God'" (Psalm 14:1). A fool may be described as a person of unsound mind. In this sense, Communism is less a philosophy than it is a reflection of a form of mental disruption or even insanity. We should never forget that.

In fact, I recently wrote a book called *Seven Men Who Rule the World from the Grave*. One of these men is Karl Marx. Marx's influence in our century has been incalculable. Marxism has enslaved half the world and (as Solzhenitsyn and others have noted) sent up to 100 million people to an early grave.

Why didn't someone stand up at the budding stages of Karl Marx's career—when this man was spouting atheism, economic determinism, dialetical materialism—and say, "Bunk! It is not true! Your philosophy is false and destructive!" The world has suffered a terrible cost for not having had the courage to oppose a philosophy that should have been rejected from the start.

Ankerberg: Dr. Breese, why is Russia even interested in the Middle East?

Breese: Well, there are several reasons for Russia's interest. First, there is tremendous wealth in the Middle East. In fact, this was the provocation for the recent battles, the tremendous oil supply.

Second, there is great mineral wealth in the Dead Sea. Third, Genesis 2:11 talks about Havilah, a land "where there is gold, and the gold of that land is good." I believe that land is somewhere in the middle of the state of Israel.

Now, just suppose this gold supply were found. Suppose it were the world's richest supply of gold—far exceeding the reserves of any nation or combination of nations. Being an economically devastated country, Russia might be tempted to grab that wealth, thereby becoming the economic master of the earth.

And fourth, we must remember that Russia has a score to settle with Israel. Not many people today realize that Russian surrogates have fought five wars against the nation of Israel. But their tanks didn't have a reverse gear. As a result, the best of Soviet armament was discredited. Consider the tanks in the last war. Our M1-A1 tanks ran rings around them.

By the way, let me illustrate the providence of God in the last war. The Iraqis set 600 oil fields afire, but four hours after they did it, the wind changed and that greasy smoke settled on the thermal sensors of the Russian tanks, totally blinding them. So our guys, coming in from the fresh air, were able to destroy the Iraqis' tanks one after another. Man may do what he will, but he can't make the wind change! I think there are spiritual lessons to be learned from that. In the end it is God's will that will be done.

Ankerberg: Dave Hunt, you have written in your book that according to Scripture, you think current events reveal that the ground is now being laid for the emergence of the Antichrist. This is the person that will lead the world, along with the False Prophet. Tell us what you mean.

Hunt: Well after all this gloom and doom that these guys have been giving us, you know . . .

Breese: Gloom, but no doom.

Hunt: . . . wars, and rumors of wars.

Breese: No, it's the other way—doom, but no gloom.

Ankerberg: Well, I don't know about you, but I'm not going to be here!

Breese: Folks, I have told Dave that he can have everything I have after the rapture.

Hunt: Well, I'm not worried. I'll be greeting you on the way up! Seriously, we have been talking about Russia coming down and attacking Israel. That will happen, but the prophetic picture is a little more complex than what we have discussed so far. The plot thickens, you know.

First, we are going to have peace. In 1 Thessalonians 5 it says, "When they shall say, *Peace and safety*; then sudden destruction" will come (v. 3; KJV). I'm not expecting Russia to move in and make this attack now. We're going to have a peace treaty first. The Bible says the Antichrist will guarantee peace for Israel.

But let me digress a moment. I find it absolutely fascinating to think of what's been happening in Eastern Europe. I mean it's almost beyond belief. If you read the Soviet paper *Perestroika*— and I guess not too many have read it—but way back in 1987, Gorbachev was talking about something incredible. He was talking about not just a United Europe—ten nations, the EEC [European Economic Community]—he was talking about a United Europe from the Atlantic to the Urals—a Europe that would include the land of Russia. In fact, in his paper Gorbachev said that "we are going to be a part of this United Europe." Now what is incredible is that the Warsaw Pact had their final meeting yesterday. The Warsaw Pact is now finished, dead. Even Hungary is coming into this alliance. Czechoslovakia, Romania, and Poland, are all going to be part of this.

Then when I read the reason that Gorbachev gave for Russia being a part of this new Europe, I almost fell out of my chair. Gorbachev said that people are trying to exclude the Soviet Union from this United Europe, but that they can't do that. Why? Gorbachev said, "We belong with Europe because of our Christian heritage. We are Christians."

Now, Dr. Breese, you were just commenting about Soviet atheism. Everyone knows it's written into their constitution. This is the head of world atheism, which has been trying to destroy Christianity for decades. And now the president of the U.S.S.R. and former KGB head is posing as a Christian. And where does Gorbachev go when he wants to unite his people? Not to Nashville to meet with the head of the Southern Baptist Convention! Instead, he goes to Rome to meet with the Pope. Why? The Pope has also been talking about a United Europe from the Atlantic to the Urals.

In other words, we are now seeing the revived Roman Empire beginning to come into place. Not only will the United Europe revive as a political and military entity, it will also unite as a religious entity.

Europe historically has primarily been a religious entity—and the Popes have played a big role in that. Constantine was the emperor when Europe supposedly became a Christian empire. And in a similar manner the Antichrist will be the emperor of the revived Roman Empire. We are beginning to see this come to pass—right before our very eyes.

Gorbachev made one other key point when he had his reunion with Ronald and Nancy Reagan in San Francisco. Gorbachev said, "We are heading for a new age and a new world age." He also said, and I'm quoting him verbatim, "*Tolerance* will be the Alpha and Omega of the New World Order."

Now, I find this hard to accept. He knows who the Alpha and Omega is. Gorbachev was baptized a Christian in the Russian Orthodox Church. He knows that Jesus claims to be the Alpha and Omega. And it's a slap in the face of Jesus when he says, "*Tolerance* will be the Alpha and Omega." He certainly doesn't mean tolerance for everything.

Look at the current crackdown in Russia. What he means is tolerance for everything that supports his view of Soviet interests. And he certainly doesn't mean tolerance for the exclusive claim of Jesus Christ, who said, "I am *the* way, *the* truth, and *the* life. No man comes to the Father but by me." (John 14:6; KJV).

When Gorbachev talks of Christianity, he's not talking about Bible-believing, born-again, evangelical Christianity. When he says, "We're Christians," he means something else entirely. He's talking about a Christianity that began in Rome and ultimately perverted the message of the gospel of Jesus Christ. And this false Christianity will embrace all religions and lay the foundation for an ecumenical one-world religion.

Breese: John, one thought on that. One of the astonishments of my life was when I was at *Pacem in Terris* ("Peace on Earth")— the peace conference conducted by John Paul XXIII at Rome around 1963. I listened to some of the speakers and collected news releases. It was an interesting experience. For the first time ever, I saw a call in those speeches for a rapproachement, a detente: incredibly, for a joining up of world Christianity and world Marxism.

Back then, I came away in disbelief. There was no conceivable rationale that could support such a merging. But since then such a rationale has been invented. It is called Liberation Theology.

One writer calls it the most serious problem the church has ever faced in its entire history. Liberation Theology is nothing but Marxism with a thin veneer of Christianity over the top. But under the rubric of helping humanity, it has the potential to become a rationale for the most astonishing mixture of "Christianity" and Marxism.

Ankerberg: Dr. Breese, in light of these facts about the role of the Soviet Union, what do you think the Bible wants us to keep in mind?

Breese: John, I would answer that on two levels. First, as far as man's sinfulness and its impact on human culture is concerned, we need to remember something. The Bible teaches that all this will one day be destroyed: "the world passes away and the lusts thereof" (1 John 2:17; KJV).

But then it offers a trememdous hope for each living person. Even though the world is passing away, every believer in Christ is promised, "He that doeth the will of God abides forever" (1 John 2:17; KJV). Thus, the first answer to "What hope do we have?" is the possibility of individual salvation, which comes to anyone when he or she believes the gospel of Jesus Christ. This salvation results in our inheriting everlasting life (John 3:16, 5:24; 6:47).

But I also believe that history demonstrates something else. If enough people believe in Christ, they establish a new "vortex" within society that can greatly be used of God. An illustration would be the Protestant Reformation and what has happened in America as a result of it. The Reformation helped to change the face of the world. That vortex, that gathering of people, praying and working and laboring together for Christ and His kingdom can still produce a result of which this world is not worthy. So we should never think that in the midst of our circumstances, we have all problems and no opportunity.

The opportunities are everywhere. That the wheat and the tares are growing together offers serious concerns, but Jesus said this would happen (Matthew 13:30). Today, the true church of Christ has the greatest opportunity it has ever known to make an impact on the world. Join it. That's my recommendation.

Ankerberg: Our next topic is of special interest to all of us. What will be the United States' role in end-times prophecy? We'll look at that in the next chapter.

5

The Role of the United States

Ankerberg: Does the Bible say the United States will play a part in the end times? Dr. Breese, in your books *Europe and the Prince That Shall Come?* and *Is Russia Off the Hook?*, you have given a scenario of three possible things that could happen to the United States. Paint the scenario for us.

Breese: Well, John, first of all I think that we are talking about a very vital subject because we are all Americans. The question, "What is the future of the United States?" comes very close to home. To say that this nation might be defeated or destroyed is not pleasant because it involves our hearts and homes, our land and our children.

But let me say I believe that God in His providence has uniquely blessed this nation—and I think so for two reasons. One, we are the fountainhead of evangelism for the world. Americans have produced 60 percent of the missionaries and 80 percent of the money to support them for the cause of Christ worldwide.

Second, we have been a friend to Israel. I believe that the Bible really speaks the earnest truth when it says, "I will bless them that bless thee and curse him who curses thee and all nations of the world shall be blessed because of thee" (Genesis

12; KJV). Here God is talking about Israel and its friends and the blessings that come to them.

Now, having said this, there's an interesting scenario that we have mentioned on past broadcasts concerning the Soviet invasion of Israel. Their intention is to capture Israel in the Middle East for reasons already mentioned. But let's think for a moment.

Consider any aggressive war. What are its components? There are two. First, a desirable prize. No nation goes to war without a purpose. There's always something that they want or need. The second component is the perceived absence of effective resistance. No matter how great the prize, a nation does not go to war if it thinks it may be destroyed in the process.

Why has Israel not been invaded by the Soviet Union before now? Humanly speaking, the answer is for one reason only: the might of America—America's nuclear capability and its willingness to use it.

Therefore, we must ask the question: "Where is America when Israel is being invaded by Russia?" There is not even a hint of suggestion for a role that America might play. Why not? There are several possibilities.

Possibility number one is that America may have been destroyed. I know that sounds like a very grim prediction. But the converse argument for the survival of the United States is not necessarily a strong one. Any nation that has been so blessed by God and yet turns so far from God (as American is now doing) can hardly have its national survival guaranteed.

Possibility number one, then, is that the United States becomes the object of a nuclear attack. As we noted earlier, General Colin Powell has highlighted that possibility.

The second possibility is nuclear blackmail, i.e., the very real threat of nuclear attack. One of the things the Soviets have been very interested in is warfare from "near space." It is rumored that the U.S.S.R. has perfected laser capability whereby they can detect the location of our submarines and many other things from their space stations, which are in constant orbit over the United States. If they were to deliver an ultimatum at a point when America was weak or preoccupied with a major crisis—and back it up with the threat of a nuclear attack from near space, what would we do? That's a real serious issue.

Possibility number three is that America may have been internally dissolved from its many problems. I taught a course at Columbia Bible College earlier this year on the ten critical issues of our time—and many of these could literally take Western civilization apart.

Let's mention just one: the threat of economic collapse. America is approaching $4 trillion in debt; right now it's $3.5 trillion. At 10 percent interest, that's $350 billion a year, or about a billion dollars a day just to pay the interest on the money that we owe. We are the net debtor nation of the world. (The net creditor nation is Japan; the second richest nation in the world is Germany.)

We talk about prosperity. But our current prosperity is based on borrowed money—and we are sending the bill to our grandchildren. Former Senator Barry Goldwater wrote a frightening book on this called *The Coming Breakpoint*. His conclusion is that there is the very real possibility of economic collapse of the American nation.

But we face nine or ten other very serious problems as well. There are thus human reasons why America might be taken out of the running in future world politics. But now, another possibility exists that could change everything, and I think Dave Hunt would like to make a description of that smashing event.

Hunt: Well, before I get to that one, let's give another logical possibility. I think the world is going to be united—one world. We're heading for a new world order, a one-world government. Who is to say that the United States could never join with the Soviet Union in attacking Israel? That sounds implausible now, but alliances in the world can change quickly. In fact, Zechariah 12:3 says, "All the nations of the world" will come against Israel and will be destroyed.

I found it rather interesting what was said earlier about God's statement concerning Israel: "I will bless him who blesses you; curse him who curses you." I think Saddam Hussein found out what it means to curse Israel. The consequences are real.

And I think it was in February that Israeli television ended their evening broadcast with these words: "God bless America." I think God has blessed America.

On the other hand, our sins are many as well. I think it was Ruth Graham who said years ago, "If God does not judge America He's going to have to apologize to Sodom and Gomorrah." So our day of judgment is coming also.

But the scenario we're talking about, of course, is the rapture. Now let me say that I think the rapture is a very key element that fits the pieces of the puzzle together.

We realize that the United States is unique, but I don't think we'll have as many people raptured from the United States as China, for example. There are probably 80 million Christians in China right now. They've had an incredible revival in the last few years.

During the rapture maybe 100 million people will disappear from Africa. But who are they? They're mostly coolies, street sweepers, and common laborers. The countries of NATO, however, will probably be left intact. Almost nobody will be leaving from those nations because they are, by and large, spiritually dead. Millions will leave from the Soviet Union. But, again, the ones who will be leaving are the common people, the politically impotent.

In the United States, President George Bush claims to be a born-again Christian. He may very well be. If he is, he's leaving, whether he believes in the rapture or not! His role in the new world order would be finished.

James Baker claims to be a born-again Christian. He gave the speech at a recent prayer breakfast in Washington. We've got senators, congressmen, they're in the White House, they're in the Cabinet—generals, admirals, fighter pilots, computer operators. Even if there are half as many born-again Christians, a quarter as many born-again Christians as the Gallup Poll says are here, the rapture would devastate this country. Hardly any power base would be left. We'd collapse.

At that point, my guess is that we would align more closely with the European Economic Community. So that could be one reason why the United States is not mentioned in biblical prophecy.

Breese: In the last analysis, the survival of a nation depends on spiritual realities. The question "What about the future of America?" depends on the "yes" or "no" answer to another issue. The Bible teaches "Blessed is the nation whose God is the Lord and the people whom he hath chosen for his own inheritance" (Psalm 33:12; KJV). If the American nation embraces the Lord with a tremendous revival, the possibilities could be fantastic. If not, we may not be long for this world.

Ankerberg: Dave Hunt, what advice would you give to people who are faced with these momentous possibilities concerning our nation?

Hunt: Well, I think the rapture of all Christians is near. I think Christ could come at any moment. But even if we suppose His return isn't near, it changes little. Our lives are in God's hands, not ours.

I shudder when I travel to various churches and the pastor begins to tell me of his great plans five or ten years down the road, fifteen years down the road. Personally, I don't even talk about tomorrow without saying, "Unless the Lord tarries," or, "Unless the Lord spares me" (James 4:13-15).

From the very beginning, Jesus said to His disciples, "Let your loins be girded about and your lights burning; and ye yourselves like unto men that wait for their Lord" (Luke 12:35-36; KJV). In Matthew 24:48 He said, "But and if that evil servant shall say in his heart, My Lord delayeth his coming. . . .'" Here evil is associated with the thought that there could be a delay.

Why? Because it's that hope of the imminent return of Christ that causes us to purify our lives. Paul wrote in 2 Timothy

4:8: "Henceforth there is laid up for me a crown of righteousness, which the Lord, the righteous judge, shall give to me at that day: and not to me only but unto all them also that love his appearing" (KJV).

In 1 Thessalonians chapter 1, verses 9 and 10, he said, I know you're Christians, not only because you're turning to God from idols to serve the living and the true God, but you are waiting for his Son from heaven. Now, would you go over to the airport and wait for Aunt Jane tomorrow if she says she's not coming for six months? Of course not! And Hebrews chapter 9, verse 28 says, "Unto them that look for him shall he appear" (KJV).

Now, I don't believe in a partial rapture. I don't believe you must be watching or Jesus won't take you. I believe that true believers are watching and waiting for Jesus Christ and that this ought to be our attitude right now.

Ankerberg: Dr. Breese, do you think we are the generation that will see the unfolding of these events, that we will be the ones who will be raptured?

Breese: You know, people today say, "Yes, I believe Christ is coming, but not now, not in this generation." My question is, "Why not?" Why couldn't it be this generation?

Christ Himself tied His return to a specific generation. "Jerusalem shall be trodden down of the Gentiles until the times of the Gentiles be fulfilled" (Luke 21:24; KJV). In verse 32, "This generation shall not pass away." Generation means the "born ones." So the suggestion is that those who are alive and see Jerusalem in Jewish hands again will see the return of the Lord.

And may I say something else that comes out of the Mid-East War in exactly that context. Isaiah 13:5-6 says that an array of great nations will gather against Babylon, and they will be there for the destruction of Babylon. And what does the next verse say? "Wail, for the day of the Lord is at hand" (NKJV*). He ties it to an assembly of great nations coming against Babylon.

Do we still have our eschatology straight? First, there is the Church Age, then the rapture, then the Day of the Lord. "The Day of the Lord is very near" in Isaiah's words. From our point of view as Christians, that means the *rapture* is at hand, which *begins* the Day of the Lord.

We do have a particular combination of events going on in our time, which any thinking person would be foolish to ignore. These events relate to what will happen at the consummation of history.

In brief, my answer is: this is the generation that should look up and allow for the possibility that *we* will be caught up into the arms of Jesus Christ. It may be today. It may be tonight. Why not?

New King James Version.

6

The Return of Jesus Christ

Ankerberg: Are the events taking place in the Middle East and around the world part of the cataclysmic world events that Jesus taught would signal His return? What specific signs did Jesus give to us that would indicate we are in the end times—that His return to earth was near?

We all realize that many people both outside and inside the church are skeptical about anyone who says signs in the Bible concerning end times apply to our generation. But, Dave Hunt, I was fascinated that in your book you responded to the skeptics' questions when you said, "There are some things that are unique to our generation. If any person will read the Bible now and look at the signs that Jesus was talking about, he will realize that these signs have never been applicable to any other generation than ours." Dave, tell us what you mean.

Hunt: First, in Matthew 24:21, 22, Jesus said there would be great tribulation that had never occurred before nor ever would again. Verse 22 says, "And except those days should be shortened, there should no flesh saved" (KJV). In any generation before ours, no one could understand that prophecy. It would have been impossible to destroy all the people on earth with bows and arrows and swords and spears. It couldn't even be done with the conventional weapons of World War II. But our generation is the first generation in the history of the world that has the weapons—not just the nuclear weapons but biological and chemical weapons—that could turn planet Earth into a sterile bit of dust drifting through space—a dead orb with no life on it at all. This prophecy didn't make sense in any generation except ours.

Second, consider Revelation 13, verses 16 and 17. It says, "He causes all, both small and great, rich and poor . . . to receive a mark . . . and . . . no one may buy or sell, except one who has the mark" (KJV). Until today, the world never had the capability of controlling all banking and commerce—all buying and selling. This could never have happened in any previous generation. It would make no sense to say such a thing could ever occur.

But in our generation it does makes sense. Today we have electronic data processing; we have extremely sophisticated computers that can speak to each other from all over the world; and we have technical marvels we call communications satellites. The whole thing is set up; everyone knows we're moving in that direction.

Third, in Revelation 13, verse 4, we are told, "They worshipped the dragon [Satan] which gave power" to the Antichrist (KJV). The whole world is going to worship Satan! That's what it says. No one could even imagine that in previous generations. But today, Satan worship is one of the fastest growing religious movements among young people.

Fourth, in Revelation 13, verse 8, referring to the Antichrist as well, it tells us, "All who dwell on the earth will worship him" (NKJV). The whole world will worship a man! Who could have believed it? That just didn't make sense.

But in our own generation the gurus have come to the West—the god-men from India—Maharishi Mahesh Yogi, Muktananda, Rajneesh, Sai Baba, and many others. Millions of people have worshiped them. Many of us have seen people bowing down and worshiping these men as God. So it is no longer inconceivable that a world united as one could worship a man—especially if he already ruled that world, if he claimed to be God, and if he performed miracles to prove it.

But we can go on and on. These are only some of the things that never made sense in any generation before ours. Today they make sense. And that makes our generation unlike any other as far as Bible prophecy is concerned.

Ankerberg: Dr. Breese, you have also written a book and you've talked about these signs. Tell us about them.

Breese: Well, John, let me respond first to the skeptics. The Bible assures us that we have in Scripture a more sure word of prophecy and that we would do well to take heed to it as we would to a light that shines in a dark place (2 Peter 1:19).

There is only one way we can know the future and that is to look into God's prophetic Word. That Word informs us that Christ's second coming will cast shadows before it.

But let me digress a moment to speak of the rapture of the church, which is surely one sign of Christ's return—and how the events of today point in the direction of the rapture's soon occurrence. When we think of the return of Christ, we need to think of His return in two senses: first of all, the rapture—Christ comes at the end of the Church Age *for* His church and the body of Christ is taken out of the world to heaven (1 Thessalonians 4:16-17). This period is succeeded by the Tribulation period, which is the first part of the Day of the Lord. At the end of that seven-year period of Tribulation, Christ comes *with* His saints at His second coming (2 Thessalonians 2:1-8).

But when He comes *for* His saints, referring to the rapture, Paul says:

> The Lord himself shall descend from heaven with a shout, with the voice of the archangel, and with the trump of God: and the dead in Christ shall rise first: Then we who are alive and remain shall be caught up together with them in the clouds, to meet the Lord in the air: and so shall we ever be with the Lord. (1 Thessalonians 4:16-17; KJV)

In other words, there will be a generation of Christians that will not die. "Behold I show you a mystery. We shall not all sleep but we shall all be changed, in a moment, in the twinkling of an eye" (1 Corinthians 15:51-52; KJV).

What does all this mean? It means this. Even though we look forward to the *rapture of the church* (the time when the Body of Christ is taken out of the world), we must remember that the signs given to us in Scripture basically apply to the second coming—the return of Christ in power and great glory.

Thus, as some have said, "If Christmas is coming, Thanksgiving is coming sooner"—that is, the signs that point to those days of the Tribulation certainly imply that the rapture, coming sooner, should be the object of our expectation.

Further, let me mention several signs that Christ spoke of in Matthew 24. The disciples approached Him and they asked, "What shall be the sign of thy coming and of the end of the world?" (KJV).

Jesus answered, "Many shall come in my name saying, 'I am the Christ' " (KJV). In other words, there will be the possibility of false Christs and religious subversion at all times.

Second, He said that there would "be wars and rumors of wars," a constantly unstable social structure. But then He mentioned additional signs characterizing the beginning of sorrows: "Nation shall rise against nation"—the Greek word in this phrase is *ethnos*. It means "racial warfare."

The next phrase in Scripture says, "kingdom shall rise against kingdom"—in other words, wars between political entities. Then there would be "famines, and pestilences, and earthquakes."

We used to think these things were beyond us because we live in a modern society. But they aren't. Take "pestilence." Even medical science with all its advancements now faces the AIDS epidemic. This alone has now killed more than 100,000 (mostly homosexual) people in America.

In Luke 21:24, Jesus also said that "Jerusalem shall be trodden down of the Gentiles until the times of the Gentiles be fulfilled" (KJV).

Christ went on to say, "When you see these things begin to come to pass, then look up, and lift up your heads; for your redemption draw[s] nigh" (Luke 21:28). Because of all these signs, we should be anticipating—and living our lives accordingly—in light of the possibility of the rapture of the church, which could take place even today.

Ankerberg: In a moment I am going to ask you, Dave Breese, "How important is this to the person that doesn't know Christ?" What impact should this information have on Christians? Why is this information important to them?" Before I do this, let me comment on the return of Jesus Christ.

General Douglas MacArthur, as he was leaving the beaches of the Philippines, once said to the Philippine people, "I will return." He kept that promise.

Jesus Christ, while He was on earth said, "I will return." And He'll keep that promise too. How do we know? Because in the Old Testament God promised certain things about Christ's first coming that were precisely fulfilled.

- For example, God foretold 700 years before He was born that the Messiah would be born of a virgin (Isaiah 7:14).

- In Micah 5:2, He said the Messiah would be born in the town of Bethlehem.

- God also said in Malachi 3 that there would be one who would be His forerunner, His announcer, John the Baptist (Matthew 11:10).

- The nature of the Messiah's work on this planet was described in Isaiah, chapters 6 and 53.

- The exact time of the Messiah's death was given to Daniel 550 years before He was even born (Daniel 9:24-27).

- God even prophesied in Scripture that the Messiah's own people would reject Him (Isaiah 53:3; John 1:11).

- He would be crucified with sinners. He would be buried in a rich man's grave. But his body would not rot in the grave—He would come back to life again, all of which was prophesied in Isaiah 53.

Every one of these prophecies was predicted about Jesus' first coming, and they all came true. If so, then, what Jesus spoke concerning His second coming will also come true. Why? Because the same God who made the predictions about Christ's first coming has spoken about those events which will take place at His second coming.

But there is going to be a difference, isn't there? The first time that Jesus came, He came as the man of sorrows; the second time He's going to come as the glorified Son of God. The first time He came as the Lamb of God; the next time He is going to come as the Lion of Judah. The first time He came as the Prince of Peace; the next time He'll come as the Lord of Lords. Nineteen hundred years ago He came to give His life a ransom for many; the second time He will come as the author and finisher of our faith. The first time He came to atone for lost sinners; the next time He's going to come to judge them. The first time He humbled Himself as a servant and was despised; at His second coming He shall come with clouds of glory and great power, and every knee shall bow before Him.

Dave, what do you say to the person who is not a Christian, to someone reading about these prophecies?

Breese: Well, John, I would tell them that the second coming is as certain as Christ's own resurrection. Easter is a marvelous time of the year to remember the resurrection of Jesus Christ, which itself was a fulfillment of prophecy. Jesus said, Destroy this tabernacle, I'll raise it up again in three days (Mark 14:58). Christ also promised, Because I live, you too shall live (John 14:19). This is extremely relevant to any person who is not sure whether he or she knows Christ. The purpose of the prophetic Word is to bring people the truth of the gospel, that Christ died for their sins and rose again. The resurrection of Christ is relevant to any person who is within the sound of this voice.

For if a person believes that Jesus Christ is the Son of God, that He died for their sins on the cross, was buried, that He rose again the third day, and if that person receives Christ as his personal Savior, he is instantly and eternally saved. So, by believing in the resurrection of Christ, a person has God's gift of everlasting life.

So, I would advise any person, if he's not sure he's saved, to just say that wonderful "yes" to Christ and be saved. Then, when He comes again, that person can know that they're going to be with Him.

Ankerberg: Dave Hunt, why is this information important to the Christian?

Hunt: Jesus didn't rise from the dead to float off into space somewhere. He said He's coming again. You just quoted Him on that subject. The return of Jesus Christ is integral to Christianity, the very faith that we have embraced as believers in Jesus Christ. We can no more ignore His promise to return than we can ignore anything else in Scripture. He said, "If I go and prepare a place for you, I will come again and receive you unto myself" (John 14:3; KJV).

The very heart of Christianity is celebrated during the time of communion. At that time we meet together to take the bread and the wine in remembrance of the death, burial, and resurrection of Jesus Christ: "As often as you eat this bread and drink this cup, you proclaim the Lord's death till He comes" (1 Corinthians 11:26). That's the heart of Christianity, the hope of the return of Jesus Christ; that's what motivated the dedicated lives of the early Christians.

For example, Philippians 3:20 says, "Our citizenship is in heaven, from whence also we look for our Savior, the Lord Jesus Christ." God tells us He's going to come back. That is why we are looking for Him. Or at least, we should be. And that should motivate our lives. We don't have time to dillydally. We've got to be witnesses for Him; we've got to live for Him, and we ought to do it now because He can come at any moment.

Ankerberg: Dr. David Breese and Dave Hunt, we want to say thank you to both of you for the information you've given us. We're also grateful for all the time and study that you've put into your books, which have challenged us. Thank you for being our guests. Good night and God bless you.

Part II
Some of the Coming Events in God's Prophetic Agenda

Introduction

Part Two contains excerpts from a private interview conducted after the telecast "Current World Events and Biblical Prophecy." Once again the participants, along with John Ankerberg, were David Breese and Dave Hunt.

7
The Coming One-World Government

Ankerberg: George Bush says he is going to create a new world order. What do you think he will accomplish, and how do you think that will fit into the prophetic picture?

Hunt: Well, I'm not a prognosticator, but I think he may very well accomplish a great deal. I think one of the reasons is that right now we've got the ball rolling in the Middle East. The Coalition built in the Gulf War is still together and involves Arabs as well as Westerners. Europe does about $10 billion a year with Israel, and they have already threatened to cut Israel off if they don't make peace with the Arabs. I don't think Israel can afford that.

On the other hand, Israel is very stubborn. So I think there are going to have to be some concessions on both sides. I think that the Arabs will be more ready now to make concessions since they've just had infidels in there protecting Mecca and Medina. So I think Bush has the momentum and has demonstrated his ability as an international leader to be able to put things together. I would give him a pretty good chance of pulling something off. But it could take time.

Ankerberg: Is President Bush going to be able to force a settlement on Israel via Europe and the rest of the Arab countries?

Hunt: I don't think it's going to be by force. The Israelis have made that very clear. You don't force them to do anything. But they are reasonable. And if they can get recognition that they've never had before, namely, their right to exist as a nation, then they will make a deal. If they do, I think that will pull the rug out from under Islam, because the Koran says that Israel has no right to exist. So that agreement is going to be tough to get. But if the Arabs are willing to recognize Israel, I think Israel could very well give them some land. They will compromise. Israel won't give them everything they want, but they might give them something if they have assurances.

Ankerberg: We went from the high emotion of world peace and the fall of Communism last summer—then the very next month— to the invasion of Kuwait, where the whole world watched as we quickly armed Saudi Arabia. We went from the heights to the depths in terms of emotion.

Could that happen again soon? Isn't this region still a tinderbox? Didn't we just sell—I think it was—$950 million worth of new Patriot missiles to Israel?

U. S. News and World Report said that Syria has been armed even further than Iraq before Iraq invaded Kuwait. Saudi Arabia has just put in a shopping list for the latest armaments. Now the KGB is taking over what seems to be the vacuum that's being left with the turmoil in Russia. Then there's the emergence of Europe coming up. And we still have Qaddafi, Arafat, and other terrorists running around the Middle East. Inside Israel the Palestinians themselves aren't getting any happier. Jordan is continuing to meet with some of the leaders that didn't go with the Coalition. It seems as if there are too many ingredients that remain as loose ends. With a very quick shift somewhere, the tinderbox could be ignited again, and where would that lead us?

Breese: First of all, I don't think the Mideast War is over. You still have a nation called Iraq. You still have Israel, who feels that it hasn't produced the proper retribution for the attacks against her. You still have the Soviet Union, who attempted to muscle in on the arrangements there. So that's the beginning of a tinderbox, and then you have all the other nations that you mentioned.

Ankerberg: Do you think Israel is going to retaliate now that the war is over?

Breese: I do. I think that the best possibility is that the remaining insanity of Iraq may cause Hussein, perhaps as his last gasp, to order all the remaining SCUD missiles fired at Israel. That, I think, is one of the real possibilities. And I think that you have the highest potential of any place in the world now for a nuclear retaliation, Israel against Iraq.

I think that we should note that the Scripture says that at the sound of the destruction of Babylon the earth will tremble and the nations will be angry (Jeremiah 50:46). Both a tremendous sound and the earth shaking could be the fulfillment of that prophecy. It could also be a trigger mechanism for tremendous anger of all the nations of the world against Israel. Israel will have spoiled the world's hope for peace and therefore should bear the guilt of the emergence of the world into war again. Something like that may trigger all nations coming against Israel.

Ankerberg: Dave Hunt, do you also think Israel will retaliate against Iraq now that the war is over?

Hunt: We all know that they have the right to do so. I doubt that they will unless there is further provocation. If, as Dave says, there is a SCUD attack, then I think they would, because they wouldn't be risking the Coalition any more at this point. I don't know that Saddam is that insane. I don't think Saddam is going to last. What he's doing is horrible. The massacre that's going on. I don't think that the man can continue to remain in power.

Ankerberg: Given all the things we are discussing, how far away are we from a one-world government in your estimation?

Breese: Things are happening very fast now, so we have to keep this in mind: Consider the Berlin Wall. James Baker said three days ago, "Nobody could have predicted this event." But the first day, November 6, 1989, 100,000 came through, which astonished everyone. Then a week later a million marched through. No one could believe it. Everyone started to say, "Wow! Things are sure going fast!" Some said that "in five or ten years maybe we will finally have a United Germany." And you know Germany was united within a matter of months, not years. So I don't think it is wise to say it will take a hundred years before there is a one-world government.

Ankerberg: What else are you thinking about the time it will take to establish a one-world government?

Breese: We now have Europe coming together in 1992 as a United States of Europe. I thought that was almost a presumptuous announcement when they first made it. They announced the EEC about ten years ago, but the part about them uniting as a United States only three years ago. So it is apparent that the whole world is on the make for some new recasting of society and culture into a new mold. Unfortunately, it is Babylonish culture, a culture without God.

8
The United Nations and World Peace

Will the United Nations
Call the World to Peace?

Ankerberg: In light of the Gulf War and the part the U.N. played in forming the Coalition, has the U.N. been revived?

Breese: The U.N. has been given prestige such as it has not had in at least ten years.

Ankerberg: What are they going to do with it?

Breese: First of all, their new power is real. The president wisely deflected a lot of criticism from the world by waiting on the U.N.'s permission at every step. What will the U.N. do with its new power? It will surely meet and press its new peace mandate on the world. I think the first thing it will do is call for a world peace conference to outlaw war. That's bound to be a major event. And I think that it will be constrained to press strongly for this because it has had an inferiority complex. Someone called this the paranoia of illegitimacy.

Ankerberg: A world peace conference is bound to capture the attention of the world. But what would be the agenda, and who would lead it?

Breese: In my opinion, they will first try to establish peace in the Middle East. Then that will move quickly to a world peace conference and then to a sifting out of those things that are detrimental to world peace by those in power.

Ankerberg: That's easier said than done. What will be the U.N.'s methodology for approaching those issues? Who will step up to the lectern to lead?

Breese: It could be that the U.N. first asks for an aggregate group to flush out the issues. Then out of their animated discussion a new leader emerges who has a commanding presence.

Ankerberg: Dave Hunt, what do you think?

Hunt: It will be a new world order because it's never been done before. Aggressors are no longer permitted because it's a new world order. There are new rules now.

Ankerberg: You've thought about the U.N. Do you agree that the U.N. has been revived and will be a main part of the scenario?

Hunt: Definitely. I don't know what it will ultimately develop into, but everything is there in place. And no one can argue that the U.N. did function superbly in the Gulf War. They were united. They voted sanctions and a remedy for a difficult situation. So I think the U.N.'s power has now been revived. It's prestige is raised.

But this new search for peace will fail because it does not address the real cause of conflict and war. The evil of man's heart is going to prevent any true peace from being established. Isaiah 57:21 says, "There is no peace, saith my God, to the wicked" (KJV).

There is no peace possible in this world until men are right with God, until Jesus Christ is no longer left out of the picture. So if the U.N. achieves peace, it will only be a trap that plays into the hands of the Antichrist, who will take advantage of this peace and destroy many. So peace can be even more dangerous than war. In war people at least recognize their need of God, their need of help, but in global peace it could seem like we've solved our problems and we don't need God.

The Deception of the Coming World Peace

Ankerberg: Is it possible that the world's desire for peace could result in a massive political double-cross of some nations?

Breese: At this time there is the call for peace in a very specific sense. A peace conference is what they're talking about now with reference to the Middle East. But these agendas change easily. A peace conference in the Middle East would quickly turn to the question of global peace. Questions would be asked. Who are the disturbers of global peace? Israel for sure. And perhaps the U.S. The strength of the U.S. produces animosity and jealousy among envious nations.

A holistic approach would be adopted that said global peace can only be achieved through the absence of hunger and poverty, and the cure of all similar ills. But out of this call for peace could come a whole set of bankrupting pressures on nations.

Peace is a funny thing. It really means the absence of war and that makes it kind of vacuous. So the idea that we can have permanent peace is the guarantee that all the days of the future will be protected by that nebulous thing called peace. However, this is a promise that no man or nation can make.

The promise also presents dangers. I think the world has had enough war and is turning away from it. But the promise of peace will produce the danger that the world will trust the agreement sworn to on paper without any other assurances. Thus, even peace will become a tool for the Antichrist—"by peace he will destroy many." So peace actually becomes subversive. Peace is promised but only for a more sinister purpose.

Hunt: Yes, I agree.

Ankerberg: It has just been announced that now America is going to leave a contingent force in Saudi Arabia. So that has already changed things even though Bush hasn't officially revealed this.

Hunt: In the Middle East we are going to see our first regional security council. Ultimately, I think there will be ten of them throughout the world. I think that the hope for the world is more powerful if it is based on a genuine hope for peace than if it's based upon a fear of war. I think the hope for peace is really high now because of the success of the American coalition.

Ankerberg: The Gulf War produced the greatest environmental disaster of history. And no one knows the repercussions of 600-800 burning oil wells. They talk of that great cloud going across India and China, bringing famine because the sun can't get through to support the crops.

Hunt: Of course, pollution doesn't respect national boundaries. To enforce world ecology will ultimately require a one-world government.

Ankerberg: If they don't get a cap on these fires and one of Carl Sagan's predictions is correct that it may wipe out the harvests of one of those eastern countries such as India, then you would have an illustration that would strengthen the ecological movement and add additional impetus to the peace movement. What else will contribute to this false peace?

Breese: The high cost of war. The skyrocketing cost of high-tech war is bound to be a contributing factor to a false peace. When the U.S. Congress starts talking about a billion dollars a day for the war, plus a $400 billion deficit this year and a $3.5 trillion debt, there will be new cries of agony. The world is fast realizing that war is just too expensive. War costs too much. And after all, all that money could have gone to feed to the poor and for so many other needed things.

9
The Pope and the United Nations

Ankerberg: How Does the Pope fit into the scheme of world unity?

Breese: A united Europe will have enormous economic capability. Europe has the best diplomats, the longest history, and they harbor ambitions far beyond any initial phase of a United States of Europe. But even the Pope has called for Europe to return to the "old" values, referring to a kind of Holy Roman Empire.

Ankerberg: What is the relationship of the Pope to the EC [European Community] and the 1992 situation?

Breese: The Pope has gained more respect than any Pope has had in the memory of people. He has tended not only to put the Vatican on the map but really to represent the old values of Europe. Even Malachi Martin thinks that, given the Bible's teaching about the Antichrist, a United Europe with the Vatican in the middle is the most likely base for establishing a world religious unity.

Hunt: Robert Muller, who recently retired as U.N. Assistant Secretary General, agrees with this sentiment. He believes the hope of the world is not just the United Nations. It is a coalition between the U.N. and all the religions of the world joining together. And he hopes that before the year 2000 the Pope himself will address the U.N. from the standpoint of the ecumenical union of the world's religions.

Ankerberg: Do you think the Pope will come to urge the world to form a religious unity or to pronounce it as a fact?

Breese: Who knows? Perhaps to embody it.

Ankerberg: By the way, has an invitation to speak been extended to the Pope yet?

Hunt: Not yet. But sooner or later a man of his power can hardly fail to address the U.N. on the spiritual hope of this world and what the world must do. In other words, he will spell out how the religions of the world must unite and cooperate together for the sake of world peace.

Breese: There must be some mucilage that makes it happen— some unifying concept. I don't see that unifying concept promoted today like Hitler had with his thousand-year Reich and the superiority of the German nation. It's a vision, the selling of a dramatic, commanding vision. I think we should all watch for a future ideological contest. One that will produce a special vision. One that will be so compelling, it will galvanize the whole world to get together. It will be a kind of futurism, I think. It will be globalism. It will also require a degree of mysticism because the nuts and the bolts alone don't really inspire anybody. So I would start to listen for an emergent voice that is able to speak conceptually and cause more people than ever to say, "That's for me. I'd give my very soul for this."

Ankerberg: I don't think it would be feasible to expect the world to invite the religious leaders of one particular group, however significant, to address the world on how to unite religiously. But possibly the U.N. might ask a number of different religious leaders to come as a group and that group would elect a spokesman to represent their views to the world. And the Pope could very well be the individual chosen to be the spokesperson for them. What do you think?

Breese: Did you see the Dali Lama interviewed today?

Hunt: No, I didn't.

Breese: The Pope has a great friendship with other religious leaders, such as the Dali Lama, the head of Tibetan Buddhism. The Dali Lama was interviewed on television today. He speaks credible English and was called "Your Holiness" by the woman interviewing him.

Hunt: In fact, even the Pope calls the Dali Lama "Your Holiness."

Breese: When the reporter asked him. "What is the spiritual force that is needed in the world today?" he replied, "We need to get together with unity and love and understanding."

10

How Could the Soviet Union Successfully Conquer America?

Ankerberg: A lot of people think that Russia is kind of a has-been power right now. What do you think?

Breese: We're facing an expanded military might. They've increased their military budget this year from what it was last year, and last year from the year before. So the Soviet military is in an expansionist mode.

They are building a Typhoon-class submarine, one every forty-five days, nine per year. *Forbes* magazine carried the story that the Typhoon-class submarine is the ultimate stealth weapon. Its only purpose is to get in close enough to the shores of the United States so it can't miss.

Ankerberg: How does it work? Why is the Typhoon submarine feared so much?

Breese: They have a device that we have not entirely analyzed. As of two months ago, when this news was published, the submarine appeared to have a round affair that sticks up almost like a jet engine. The submarine is feared because it is silent running and therefore undetectable. That is where the ultimate stealth comes from. If these submarines were to get in close enough to the United States and took out even one city, the Soviet Union could blackmail us after that. They could inform us that unless we wanted to lose all our cities, we must surrender immediately. It is reported that from their-near space capability and laser detection systems they now have a higher capability of discovering our submarines than we have of discovering theirs.

Ankerberg: Are you saying we have no way of protecting ourselves against their new technology?

Breese: That's right. Despite what some say, we do not have a way to protect ourselves against a well-designed attack. They have SS-18 missiles with fourteen warheads on each missile. Now, if they were fired at us and those warheads took out our land-based ICBM system, the Minutemen 3, all of the locations of which are known, what options would we have?

I visited a launch control facility in America a few years ago. I went through the security clearance and the whole thing. You go down seventy feet below ground. It's dark and the lights are gleaming and blinking on the missiles. The computer interrogates the Minuteman 3 missile in terms of seventy different circuits or so—temperature, humidity, readiness of all kinds. Then, there are six buttons over to the side. He said when it gets down to that, when we press those last six buttons and when they are all red, the missiles are flying.

I discovered they had just gone to an aiming system called the Command Data Buffer System. Up until that system they could only input six, seven, or eight targets as possibilities. But now with this new system they are able to input into the control any longitude and latitude on the face of the earth so it can be fired at an infinity of targets.

But if the Typhoon-class submarines of the Soviet Union took out our 1,050 ICBMs, what would we do to retaliate? We have only two possibilities: the seaborne missiles and B-52s. We could include the B-1, but right now it's not possible.

Well, B-52s are quite obsolete; they would be taken out quickly. Incidentally our B-52s that carry cruise missiles, by our own agreements internationally, have a special strake on the wing. This tells the ground radar which one of our planes is the most dangerous, identifying the ones carrying the cruise missiles. So, we have in advance identified those weapons for them. But anyway, could we retaliate with B-52s? No.

The next question is, would we retaliate with our submarines, which are "counter value" but not "counter force," meaning they are not accurate enough to take out military installations but only population centers? Well, think for a moment. Not having lost our population centers, would we take out Russia's population centers, knowing that they would retain the capability to take out all of ours? In all probability, no. Mutually-assured destruction would prevent that. That's why SDI is so important.

So they have the capability to destroy us, and we do not really advocate the possibility of destroying them. So that combination of things—an expanded military, the Typhoon-class submarine, the SS-24 and SS-25 missiles, and a state of expanded readiness—according to our leading military officer and Chairman of the Joint Chiefs of Staff Colin Powell—puts them in the position where they are the only nation in the world that could defeat the United States and do it in thirty minutes.

Ankerberg: What would cause the Soviet Union to risk attacking the United States?

Breese: One, a desirable prize, namely, taking the world. We are the only genuine opposition to their intentions of world conquest. And two, if they could produce a successful first strike and take out our missiles, the risk would be gone. Then they would have it all. Their attack on the Middle East would be done with impunity, because the only thing down through the years that has protected Israel has been the United States.

Ankerberg: Do you think the food crisis, the economic crisis, and their social chaos will push the Soviets to action?

Breese: I don't think so. I don't think that has anything to do with anything. They will just kill everybody that objects. A .357 Magnum beats a royal flush anytime. Those of their own citizens who object may soon be silenced. If they wanted to, the Communist leaders would be glad to give you Tiananmen Square all over again. They've already been doing this in Latvia, you know. Latvia is just a little smaller, but they've been running over people with tanks there.

So forget all that Perestroika and Glastnost stuff—it is pure propaganda. The Soviet leaders are cynical materialists for whom the only issue is what produces advantages militarily or any other way.

At least that's the best way to prepare for what they might eventually do. The way to handle a dictatorship is to never, ever, ever, ever, ever believe what they say—it's always propaganda. Rather, always realize what they can do, and depending on that, you must prepare to defend yourself. Do not listen only to an enemy's promises but evaluate his capability.

Hunt: But isn't there one slight flaw in this? The Soviets have had this capability for years. Why haven't they used it before? What are they waiting for?

Breese: Why haven't they used it up until now? I'll give you an opinion on that. For the last forty years, they have, number one, had quite good success at subversion, and they've been able to take all of Eastern Europe without a direct military conflict. So they have depended upon propaganda and subversion for the taking of nations, which is a lot cheaper that fighting a war.

Hunt: But wouldn't nuclear blackmail be quicker and easier?

Breese: But nuclear blackmail has dangers in it that are not in subversion. The Soviets feel that time is on their side. Communism has called itself the wave of the future. Second, they have perceived their military capability in comparison to that of the West as expanding. Because of this time has, in their mind, worked on their side. But now the Gulf War and the astonishing revelation of American technology must convince them that America has an insuperable technological advantage. Therefore, what their attitude, in my opinion, must be is to see if there is a window of opportunity closing, whether they will speak now or forever hold their peace. If the window of opportunity closes, they realize it is all over. They will be forced to deal with domestic problems, which they have not yet been able to handle.

Hunt: Let me play the role of the devil's advocate on this, Dave. Can we say that Glasnost and Perestroika are not for real? It would seem then that they've gone an awfully long distance in the direction of discrediting Communism. I don't see why all that was necessary—of relinquishing their control of Eastern Europe and so forth, and acknowledging before the world that Communism doesn't work—if it is all a smoke screen. Now why would they do that?

Breese: Because Communism never did work.

Hunt: Right. But what was their purpose for losing control. It seems to me that Gorbachev has meticulously gone about dismantling this whole thing that Lenin successfully built up.

Breese: No. He hasn't dismantled anything.

Hunt: As far as its credibility and its hold on the people he has. And now they're allowing demonstrations in the streets of Russia.

Breese: Yes, but the substantive thing is, who's got the gun? That's the substantive thing. The rest is applesauce.

Hunt: It wasn't a matter of guns in Eastern Europe though, it was students marching in the streets.

Breese: Yes, but they could have retained anything in Eastern Europe with the troops they have there. The question always with a dictatorship is firepower, military capability. And the rest, the demonstrations in the streets, in my opinion, are not to be discounted, but they are not the final word.

I think we are watching an amazing phenomenon. I think there is an opportunity for the gospel that is ours with reference to the Soviet Union and Eastern Europe and all the rest of it. It is utterly fantastic. And I'm not arguing against any of that being real and the power of Glastnost in that sense, but the ultimate question always is, Do they dissolve their military structure? If they don't, then they've got a tank behind the door even though they've got an idyllic picture on the front.

Hunt: What you've outlined is the KGB scenario presented by the highest KGB defector in 1984. He says the Soviets are going to give back Eastern Europe; they're going to let the wall come down; they're going to let the Western World pick up the tab and bankrupt them. His scenario is frightening. Their idea was to get the West disarmed, you know, so that we trust them and so forth. But it doesn't seem to me that they've been following that scenario. The West is not going to trust them now because of what they've done in the Baltics.

Breese: Yes, Lithuania, Latvia, etc.

Hunt: I'll tell you what I personally think, and again, I could be totally wrong. I think Gorbachev had his own agenda. I think Gorbachev would like to be world ruler. I think that he used the KGB plan Anatoly Golitsyn revealed, but the plan got away from them. Now his people are saying, "What in the world are you doing?" His response is, "Well, this was our program." But I think it's gone beyond the point where the KGB can recover. Now nuclear blackmail—I see that as an option. But I still ask, if this was their plan, why didn't they use nuclear blackmail sooner? Why go this far with all of this disruption?

Ankerberg: Take it one step at a time. I don't think the KGB will come out and threaten America right now. First of all, don't you think they will try to recover control of the country? Soon I expect to see *U.S. News & World Report* telling us Yeltzin's off the scene and Gorbachev has put certain KGB personnel into ideal places of power in the government, and those guys will basically run everything in the Soviet Union. Then you're all set up again for whatever else they would decide. They would then have all the Soviet power at their disposal.

Breese: The future biblical scenario, the way it will work out, is Russia will someday move with their own army to the Middle East and attempt to conquer the nation of Israel.

Ankerberg: But if that's true, something must have happened to the U.S. in order for them to move against Israel. What happened?

Hunt: Well, I think that's what Armageddon is all about. The Bible says the whole world is going to go against Israel and to me that includes the U.S.

Breese: Yes, that's a frightening thing: the whole world against Israel. The strong point I would make is that what keeps the Soviet Union, and what has kept them, from moving against the state of Israel has been the American military capability and our willingness to use it. Let's face it, but for the American military power any nation in the West could be conquered on the telephone. This is a fantastic consequence.

Ankerberg: So what is your scenario of why the U.S. in the future will not oppose the Soviet Union's move against Israel?

Breese: The possibilities might include an attack on the U.S. that would leave us either destroyed or greatly reduced or intimidated. In fact, realistic business leaders of the eastern Atlantic area think—this was maybe five years ago—that there is the highest possibility of a Soviet attack on one city, New York. It would take out the business leadership but not the industrial potential. It would intimidate America. Also, the nuclear fallout would go into the Atlantic Ocean, so there would be a minimum of Strontium 90 hanging around. They would have the U.S. with its potential but without its bravado. I thought that to be interesting. This was a representation of the best thoughts of men who weren't looking at it from a spiritual prophetic point of view at all.

Hunt: When the Soviet Union's missiles go into the air, won't ours go up to retaliate? I don't see how they could take out New York City.

Breese: Yes, the "launch on warning" doctrine is still being debated. Will America go with launch on warning? The left says that's a very dangerous thing because you don't know if it's an experiment or what. And once they achieve the apogee and they're coming down, it would take SDI—to which the liberals are also opposed—to stop them, so . . .

Hunt: Are you saying nuclear bombs, missiles, will come in on America and we will do nothing?

Breese: First, you have a tremendous confidence in the readiness of the U.S. to interpret an attack as an attack. Every year there have been two or three false alerts that have happened. Each alert has turned out to be a defective computer program, etc. I would not stand and put my hand in the fire to say that America would launch an all-out attack on the Soviet Union based on an alert. It would take about thirty minutes for the missile to get here based on an unidentified possible strike against us. I'm a little more confident now of U.S. capabilities, given Schwartzkopf and the present American military leadership.

Ankerberg: Back to the scenario. If it's still an unlikely scenario for Russia to launch an attack on Israel because of America, what happened to America?

Breese: As I have said, the Soviets' window of opportunity is closing. The only advantages they have now are the Typhoon-class submarines, the deadly SS-18, and our absence of SDI defense. We could modify the Patriot missile to make it ICBM capable. But the Soviets may feel that we are about to do that, and then they will lose their last genuine opportunity at world conquest. That may motivate them to act soon.

Hunt: I think Russia, as well as the Arabs, are afraid to attack Israel. Never mind the capabilities of the U.S. I mean, Israel is so potent now in its own right, and I think it's ultimately going to take all the nations of the world to have enough guts to go after that little nation.

Breese: I think that that scenario about Israel's mounting capability is, in fact, the case.

Hunt: And remember, Israel has nuclear capabilities too.

Breese: Of course. People ask me, "Do the Jews have nuclear missiles?" Well, heavens, they invented it in the first place.

Ankerberg: Has there been proof of how far they have gone in terms of their nuclear capability? What's been published?

Breese: Well, it has been said that it is estimated that they have 150 atomic—I don't know if we can use the word "hydrogen"—warheads. I asked one of Israel's military men, "What would you do if you were attacked by 50 million Arabs? And if the U.S. didn't want to come to protect you, what would you do?" He said, "The Arabs will not attack because they know that their leading cities would go up in flames." And I said, "Does that mean you have nuclear capability and are willing to admit it?" He said, "We do not say. It is better for them not to know."

Hunt: Have you read *By Way of Deception—The Making and Unmaking of a Massad Agent?* In that book he tells you about Israel's nuclear missiles. They've got them. There's no doubt about it.

Ankerberg: Let me ask you, Dr. Breese, hearing Dave Hunt's explanation about the rapture, how does that relate to our discussion?

Breese: I agree that the rapture has the potential of being a stunning event that recasts the thinking of the leaders of the world in a lot of ways. Many in positions of leadership in America will be raptured—the upper crust that are the movers and shakers, the doers—and, therefore, this will have a profound limitation on the abilities of the U.S.

After the rapture, I wonder how long it will take the rest of the world to see and understand that. I wouldn't guess that by the next day at noon the enemies of the U.S. or those who want to attack the Middle East would decide and build a strategy to do so. I really think the world will be stunned for a while.

Hunt: The Soviets will be stunned. The Kremlin will have an emergency meeting. They will realize they have lost an awful lot of people all over Russia. Because of Islam, the Arab nations won't lose but a few people.

Now, here's another speculation of mine that I haven't even mentioned in my book. God says He is not willing that any should perish. Now suppose all babies and children up to the age of accountability were taken in the rapture. Gone in an instant.

Breese: Let me get clear about what you're saying. You're talking all of the children of the world, so there are no children in the world in any land anywhere under the age of accountability that are left?

Hunt: Yes. As a result, think of the impact such an event would have on the Arab world, in China, India . . . everywhere. The world would be devastated. Terrorized!

Breese: Yes. Charles Spurgeon held that there would be more people in heaven than in hell because of infant mortality.

Hunt: Here is why I bring this up. It has to do with this bringing the world together. We've talked about the economic, political, military reasons. We've talked about agreements and coalitions and treaties and all that. I still don't think that these will unite the world. It's going to take something of horrific dimensions.

11
The Rebuilding of the Temple

Ankerberg: It seems to me that there are four important prophetic signs concerning Israel that the Bible gives us. First, the Jews will be gathered from the nations. Second, they will establish their own nation once again. Third, the Jews will possess their Holy City of Jerusalem again, and that took place in 1967. Fourth, they will someday rebuild the Temple. Dr. Breese, how do you view the significance of Israel in light of prophecy?

Breese: Up until 1967 Israel held a major portion of Palestine but not the Holy City. At that time there was the Mandelbaum Gate, the separation of Jerusalem, the barbed wires, the sand bags, and all of that. But in the '67 War, Israel possessed Jerusalem. They did so by putting their army around it, and they fought for it with hand-to-hand combat. They did this rather than risk artillery fire, which might have destroyed part of the Holy City.

After they had won the war, the Israeli army gathered at the Wailing Wall and sang a song, a verse of which was written for the occasion: "Jerusalem the Gold." Then amidst their rejoicing and celebration, General Moshe Dayan said, "Gentlemen, I promise you, we will never leave this city again."

Ankerberg: This is significant since the Bible states concerning the Jews becoming a nation, "And they shall dwell in the land that I have given unto Jacob my servant in which your fathers have dwelt and they shall dwell in it, even they and their children and their children's children *forever*" (Ezekiel 37:25; KJV).

Breese: There is another astonishing prophecy concerning Israel. It reveals there will be *a temple rebuilt in the city of Jerusalem.* We have several evidences for this in Scripture. One of them is in Daniel 9, where the Antichrist confirms the covenant with Israel for one week. In the midst of that week he causes the sacrifices and oblations to cease.

Commenting on this same event the apostle Paul says in 2 Thessalonians 2, that this evil character called the Antichrist sets himself up in the temple of God and opposes and exalts himself above all that is called God. Clearly then there must be a temple of God in the city of Jerusalem for him to profane. This is evidence that a real temple will be rebuilt.

We are now seeing terrific provocation with reference to the temple mount. In fact, the latest "intifada" upset was because people were discovered measuring the area around the Dome of the Rock. This was looked upon by suspicious Arabs as a first step in the rebuilding of the Jewish Temple, and that triggered violent action.

Ankerberg: That stone-throwing incident, you mean?

Hunt: Yes. That's been one of the big problems there. You had another fellow up there trying to blow up the Dome of the Rock.

Breese: And another one tried to burn it, too.

Hunt: And the thought has always been that somehow the Dome of the Rock, the third most holy place in the Arab world after Mecca and Medina, must be cleared in order for the Jews to build the Temple.

But now we understand that after the latest measuring, the Jews think the location for the Temple isn't really right there, and that the Temple could be built beside the Dome of the Rock. Now, it's interesting to speculate why the Muslims might be willing to actually allow that to happen.

Few Westerners realize that originally Mohammed was very much involved with Judaism. He was also acquainted somewhat with Christianity, which is why the first few chapters of the Koran coincide with some of the Bible. In fact, Islam gives an endorsement to the Bible and looks to the Bible for substantiation.

At the time of Mohammed, he had his followers pray toward Jerusalem. And they even kept the Jewish ceremony of Yom Kippur. Muslims were very good friends with Jews. This was after Mohammed had fled form Mecca to Medina and was establishing himself in Medina. He wanted to join with the Jews in kind of an ecumenical movement and make a common front against the pagans. What upset Mohammed most of all was the paganism he saw everywhere.

But the Jews didn't accept his teachings. They said Mohammed's God is not the same God. This is not the same faith. And that was what turned Mohammed against the Jews. He became very angry and slaughtered the Bani Quraizah tribe, which actually surrendered to Mohammed in good faith, but he still took the heads off of 600 men and then divided up the booty of women and children.

From that time, Mohammed began to pray toward Mecca. He also changed Yom Kippur into Ramadan. Instead of fasting for twenty-four hours for Yom Kippur, now Muslims fasted during the daylight hours for a month, the month of Ramadan. And from that time on Jerusalem had no importance to the Muslims. None whatsoever.

You know that the Muslims conquered all of that territory. They held it for centuries. And during that time nobody ever made any visits to Jerusalem. Well, if you made a visit it was called a visit, it was not called a pilgrimage. The pilgrimages were to Mecca. The rulers of Saudi Arabia never went to Jerusalem. When Jerusalem was under the control of the Jordanians, their Muslim leaders never went to Jerusalem.

The Dome of the Rock is most interesting. Inside of it, it claims to be built on the spot of El-Aqsa, which is a place mentioned in the Koran in Sura 17:1. The Koran describes it as that mystical place from which Mohammed journeyed on his horse and then went directly to heaven. But it is interesting that the Koran never identifies El-Aqsa with Jerusalem. One of the best proofs that this is not El-Aqsa is found in the Dome of the Rock itself. Of all the verses from the Koran that are printed in the Dome of the Rock, Sura 17:1 is not there.

So who gave people this idea that Jerusalem was the place from which Mohammed ascended into heaven? It was none other than the infamous Haj Amin el Husseini, the uncle of the PLO leader Yassar Arafat. Haj Amin el Husseini was the grand Mufti of Jerusalem. The SS chief Heinrich Himmler sent him cablegrams back and forth,you know, and one cablegram—you get this in the Holocaust Museum there in Jerusalem—one of the cablegrams he sent was the news that we have put into our country's plan the extermination of world Jewry.

And Haj Amin el Husseini sent back a cable to Himmler saying they were with the Axis powers in their destruction of the Jews from Europe. It is this man who finally fled to Germany and broadcast the following message back to his fellow Arabs: "Join together as one man and kill the Jews wherever you find them. This pleases God and religion and restores mankind."

So it was in the 1920s, in order to arouse the fervor of the Arabs and erect a united front against the Jews, that Haj Amin el Husseini invented the story that Jerusalem and the Dome of the Rock was the place mentioned in the Koran to be El-Aqsa. From that time on, Jerusalem began to take on great importance for the Muslims. But it was a fabrication. It was a story that Haj Amin el Husseini made up for his own political reasons.

Ankerberg: That was the first time anyone in history had identified Mount Moriah in Jerusalem as being the site of El-Aqsa?

Hunt: Right. And he did so in order to keep the Jews out of Jerusalem. So now, if this historical fact will be acknowledged by Muslim scholars and this myth is set aside, it would seem to me that it would lower the importance of Jerusalem and the Dome of the Rock enough to where they would be willing to compromise and allow a Jewish temple to be built next to it.

12
Islam, Idol Worship, and the Black Stone

Hunt: I find it fascinating that it was the pagans who first made the pilgrimages to Mecca. Have you ever seen the cabal where they walk around? It's like the porticos of a temple around it. This cabal was once a pagan temple containing idols. It was here that the idol worshipers came and made their pilgrimages. The anti-pagan, anti-idol worshiping Muslims make their pilgrimages to Mecca, and the cabal is the object of this pilgrimage. Will Durant says that when Mohammed destroyed the idols in the temple, he kept the name of the chief idol, Allah, as the name of his God. Kind of like Catholicism. We'll change the names Isis and Horace into Mary and Jesus but retain the essence. Mohammed also kept the black stone.

Ankerberg: Did you say that Mohammed destroyed all the idols but kept the pagans' sacred black stone?

Hunt: Yes, Mohammed kept the black stone. That's what the Muslims all kiss now. Before Islam it was the chief object of idolatrous worship. It had the power. The stone even today is viewed as having strong powers. And it is still there. Muslims still come to the idol temple, which is now empty of idols, except for Allah and the black stone. So today Muslims unwittingly worship the chief pagan idol of yesteryear as their God (Allah), and like the pagans they conquered, they still make their pilgrimages to Mecca to kiss the idolatrous black stone. Once these facts are known, I think this offers potential for certain ecumenical transformations in Islam.

Ankerberg: Is there anything that has affected the Muslim mind as a result of the Gulf War? For example, do Muslims in Kuwait and Iraq think Allah has let them down because they lost in war?

Hunt: For Muslims, defeat always indicated the judgment of God. Whenever they lost to the Jews, they said it was a spiritual problem. In fact, that was the impetus for this fundamentalist movement. So Muslims everywhere said, "We've got to get back to the Koran; we've got to get back to Allah; and we've got to get in a right relationship with our God—and then we will have His power." But in spite of the existence of the Fundamentalist Movement, they have lost to the infidels again.

Some tried to say, "Well, Saddam didn't represent true Islam." But then why did you have all the Islamic fundamentalists claiming Saddam as their hero? Even now they're trying to say that he won the Gulf War. This includes even the Palestinians and the PLO. So the war itself could have a shaking effect on the Muslim mind.

Breese: No one spoke more about God than did Saddam Hussein. Every day he had some speech about "God is with us" and "We will have the infidels swimming in pools of their own blood." He called the other Muslim nations, like Saudi Arabia and Egypt, insulting names, blaming them for being betrayers of the cause of Islam.

Remember his daily speech in which he said, "God is with us. We have prayed and the victory is ours"? In fact, he spoke more about Allah than any ruler in a long time, but Saddam's army was destroyed by the Western infidels, and I believe his defeat will add further disillusionment to those in Islam. It will probably cause a loss of faith and greater disillusionment.

13
False Prophets
and Counterfeit Miracles

Ankerberg: Do you think that the church is being prepared for a worldwide revival of religion that will support the Antichrist.

Hunt: The Bible says, "The time will come when they will not endure sound doctrine" (2 Timothy 4:3; KJV). We are certainly in that time frame. Not just when you've got false doctrine, which has always been present, but that they will not endure sound doctrine. In fact, some are saying that doctrine is not important anymore. Only experience.

Breese: Maybe we should also mention that one of the initial characteristics of the rise of Antichrist will be the falling away of those in the church. Consider the evidence. We have at least 300,000 churches in the U.S., and if one could find 10 percent of them that still stand for the Book and the blood and the blessed hope, that would be almost a delightful figure.

Hunt: If Martin Luther were alive today, he'd be accused of schism, not just by the Catholics but by the Protestants. The cry of the Reformers was Sola Scriptura. The Catholic church said "No sola Scriptura." We've got tradition. We've got the pronouncements of the Pope. We've got the canons and decrees of the Councils and so forth. But at least they were looking to religious pronouncements, religious leaders, bad as they might have been.

Today we've got the Christian psychologists saying, "No sola Scriptura. All truth is God's truth." They're not going to the pronouncements of the religious leaders, they're going to the Freuds and Jungs and so forth. Why not Buddha or Mary Baker Eddy, if Freud is a good source of God's truth? They've confused truth with facts of science, even if psychology were scientific.

Talk about ecumenism! It's bad enough to join conservative evangelicals with liberals, and Roman Catholics with Protestants, but how about joining Christ to Freud? This is the ultimate ecumenism.

Then one of the cries of the Reformers was against images. Today we've got worse images. We've got Protestant images today that talk to you personally. You visualize them. We've got little images of Jesus and God and everything else. There are books out there written to youth ministers giving yoga exercises and mantric breathing and so forth. Then they say, "Now visualize God. When you focus on this image, it will speak to you."

So the church is in worse shape, in my opinion, than it was in the days of the Reformation. Now, if you go to 2 Timothy 3:8, "As Jannes and Jambres withstood Moses, so do these also resist" (KJV). Resist what? The truth! "Men of corrupt minds, reprobate concerning the faith." Well, how did Jannes and Jambres, magicians in Pharaoh's court, oppose Moses? Was it skepticism, or atheism? No. Miracles! The power of Satan!

So Paul is telling us, "Do you want to know what the opposition to the truth will be in the last days?" It's not going to be atheism or skepticism, it's going to be what Jesus warned about—false prophets, false christs, who will do miracles— seeming miracles. They will be so convincing that if it were possible they would deceive the very elect.

There are some today who are doing exactly what Simon the Magician did in Acts 8. Simon sees the apostles lay hands on people and they receive the Holy Spirit, and he says, "I'll pay you money if you'll teach me the technique."

Today there are false Simons coming into towns and saying to the pastors, "If you'll pay me money, I'll teach you how to do miracles.

Pastors by the thousands are accepting this. I mean, this is sorcery that has come into the church. Some are claiming all you have to do is hold your hands out and you feel a hot spot on another person's body and that's supposed to be the Holy Ghost at work. So we've got occult techniques that are being practiced in the name of Jesus. In the church the apostasy, I think, is just horrendous. So that's another reason why I think the coming of the Lord must be very near.

Ankerberg: How can you help people discern the supernatural? Some churches are having miraculous things happen while others only claim it's miraculous. It may be miraculous, but the fact is at the same time they are also coming out with all kinds of weird, false doctrine from the "spirit" that descends on them in their meetings.

Hunt: I think it gets back to something Jesus said in John 7:17. First of all, Jesus said, "If any man wills to do God's will, he will know of the doctrine whether it be of God or whether I speak of myself" (KJV). My caution, my warning to Christians is that their heart must be right to begin with.

I can remember when as a young Christian I took Hebrews 11:6, "He who comes to God must believe that He is . . . a rewarder of them who diligently seek Him" (NKJV). And I thought, Ah-ha, that's the formula. If I diligently seek God then I'll get this Cadillac or whatever. No! If I'm seeking God, He will reward me with Himself.

The most important issue is to know God and to be an instrument of His will. Never mind whether I get crucified, whether I'm delivered, whether miracles happen through me or whatever; but first of all I must love Him and love His Word and want to know Him and do His will. If that's not right, then my motives are wrong. If I'm in this thing for the prestige or the power or the experience, the excitement, the new revelation, whatever it may be, then I will be led astray.

14

The Virgin Mary's New
Revelations to Pope John

Ankerberg: Dave, do you think the personal visions people are having of Jesus and Mary are an aspect of the very things Jesus warned us about when He said, "Many will come in My name, saying . . . 'here is the Christ!' or, [Look,] He is there!' do not believe [it]. For false Christs and false prophets will rise and show [great] signs and wonders [so as] to [mislead], if possible, even the elect" (Mark 13:6, 21-22; NKJV)?

Hunt: I think 1 Timothy 4:1 is another unique sign for our generation. "Now the Spirit speaketh expressly, that in the latter times some will depart from the faith, giving heed to seducing spirits, and doctrines of devils" (KJV).

There is no generation in the past that has actively involved itself in contacting spirit beings like our generation. This is shamanism. Remember, in his mind a shaman goes on a journey into the past or the future, into the upper or lower worlds to make contact with spirit entities and to pick up a spirit guide. And today we are literally pursuing this in the business world and in medicine. I could name numerous medical doctors and business leaders. It's also in psychology. It's in our public schools. Little kids in Nebraska are being taught to visualize themselves under water and see Doso the Dolphin coming, and how to start a conversation with him. They are promised, "He will talk to you."

But it's also in the church. People are visualizing Jesus, visualizing Mary. The image that they come up with in their mind literally talks to them. In doing so, they don't realize they have made contact with the spirit world. Today we are training ourselves to be demonized. The whole world is into this.

Another interesting part of this is in the Catholic church— The visions of Mary, for example. The Pope himself has seen Our Lady of Fatima. In fact, just as the assassin was aiming the gun at him, he saw a child with a little picture of Our Lady of Fatima. Because he leaned over to bless this child, that's why the first bullet missed his head. But after that he was wounded.

During the Pope's convalescence, he relates how he had a vision of Our Lady of Fatima. His vision convinced him that because his assassination took place on the anniversary of Our Lady of Fatima's first appearance in May 13, 1917, that the following year the Pope should make a pilgrimage to Fatima. In his vision he was instructed to go there and pray and to dedicate the world to the Immaculate Heart of Our Lady of Fatima.

There is something wrong here. First of all, the biblical Mary herself isn't the one appearing. The things that the Lady of Fatima is saying in people's visions indicate that this is a demon posing as Mary. This is an example of a seducing spirit and people following doctrines of devils.

Ankerberg: Dave, some Catholics would say that's just your Protestant opinion. What reasons can you give that prove this is really a demon posing as Mary?

Hunt: Well, Mary said that there would be no peace until this world is dedicated to "My Immaculate Heart." That contradicts Scripture. Isaiah 9:6 says that *Jesus* is the Prince of Peace. Romans 5:1 tells us, "Therefore being justified by faith, we have peace with God through our Lord Jesus Christ" (KJV; see Ezekiel 13:8-10). Yet the Mary in the Pope's vision posed as the one who is the Prince of Peace, the one who would bring peace to this world. She was even accompanied by a little Jesus, a Baby Jesus.

Now, this is wrong. I mean, Jesus was a 33-year-old man, a mature man, when He died on the cross. He is at the Father's right hand as a resurrected, glorified Savior who bears the marks of Calvary. Why would He now come as a little baby Jesus who floats on a cloud of light next to Mary?

And then this little Jesus says that until the world is dedicated to the Immaculate Heart of Mary in reparation for the sins the world has committed against her there will be no hope of peace. Mary herself told the Pope, "You must say the rosary daily in order to bring peace to the world."

All these revelations from Mary are what cause Catholic theologians to teach things like, "No one has even been saved except through your intercession, O Mary, Mother of God" (*Mary, Queen of Apostles*, p. 22, 1976). This clearly denies what the Bible teachers in Acts 4:12, that there is no other name—Jesus—given among men under heaven by which we must be saved. Again, I believe these are doctrines of devils. This is not Mary, this is not Jesus. It can only be coming from a seducing spirit because what they say contradicts biblical teaching.

Now, in Medjugorjie, Yugoslavia, as all around the world, appearances of Mary are increasing every day. So, there's a great movement now following Mary. She also has as great appeal for the women's movement, for they are looking for women who will stand for leadership and for peace. Of course, it is amazing to me to read that it is a woman who rides the beast in Revelation 17. The woman controls and directs the beast to begin with. But later he eats her flesh.

So we're having an explosion of looking to seducing spirits, making contact with them, acknowledging them. And the Pope literally believes that he is to acknowledge Mary, who appeared to him and who saved his life for a purpose. He also believes that someday she is going to give to the world a sign in the sky. The Pope believes it will be some kind of a major disruption of this world that will be so profound that all the world will recognize him as the moral and spiritual leader to whom they must now look for direction.

Ankerberg: You're talking about the present Pope?

Hunt: Yes. The present Pope believes this. He's a man waiting. He has a mission from Mary, and he's waiting for this miraculous sign to be given to him. Now, I personally think the sign will be the rapture.

Part III
Biblical Predictions Concerning
Future World Events

Introduction

The future has a habit of suddenly and dramatically becoming the present.

Roger W. Babson

I expect to spend the rest of my life in the future, so I want to be reasonably sure of what kind of future it's going to be. That is my reason for planning.

Charles F. Kettering

The Bible does predict a general pattern of events for the future. In this section, we will examine several trends that appear to integrate both biblical predictions and current world situations. We will show why these predictions are important to the future of the world and how the stage is being set for their fulfillment.

Intellectuals are usually skeptical about this kind of information. Therefore, we have taken pains to document all we say. We believe this is evidence everyone must grapple with.

We will show how current world conditions warrant the conclusion that we may be approaching the return of Christ. Once the predicted events occur, Christ's second coming is shortly inevitable. Anyone who reads prophetic Scripture literally would agree that given the current geopolitical makeup of the world, the outline of events cited is at least plausible for our lifetime.

Unlike the self-proclaimed prophets of today, the prophets of the Bible did not peddle vague and general predictions that could be adjusted to any situation. The prophecies recorded in the Bible are detailed and intricately interwoven. Although interpretation of minor points may vary, the overall picture is frighteningly clear. The Bible does not simply speak of a final destructive world war, but of a whole series of carefully timed events on a doomsday calendar leading to Armageddon. (Walvoord, *Armageddon*, p. 23)*

---

*Complete information for the partial references contained in parentheses can be found by turning to the bibliography.

15

The Return of the Jews to Palestine to Form the Nation of Israel

"Can you give me one single irrefutable proof of God?"
"Yes, your Majesty, the Jews."
Marquis D'Argens to Frederick the Great

What Are the Ancient Biblical Prophecies?

Ezekiel 37:21 (586 B.C.):

Say to them, "This is what the Sovereign Lord says: I will take the Israelites out of the nations where they have gone. I will gather them from all around and bring them back into their own land."

Ezekiel 39:27-28 (586 B.C.):

When I have brought them back from the nations and have gathered them from the countries of their enemies, I will show myself holy through them in the sight of many nations. Then they will know that I am the Lord their God, for though I sent them into exile among the nations, I will gather them to their own land, not leaving any behind. (See also Ezekiel 36:3-6, 15, 26-30, 35-36; 37:26-27; 38:17-18; 39:21-22, 27-29.)

No one can deny that Israel is again a nation after 1900 years of nonexistence. It is also evident that this little country is increasingly capturing the attention and concern of the entire world.

As early as Deuteronomy 28:64-65 (ca. 1500 B.C.) God had warned the people of the nation of Israel that if they did not obey Him, they would be scattered among the nations: "Then the Lord will scatter you among all nations, from one end of the earth to the other. . . . Among those nations you will find no repose, no resting place." This occurred twice: during the Assyrian and Babylonian captivities; and when Jerusalem was destroyed by Titus in A.D. 70, dispersing the Jews worldwide.

But in Deuteronomy 30:1-3, God also promises that He will bring the Jews back to their homeland:

> Then the Lord your God will restore your fortunes and have compassion on you and gather you again from all the nations where he scattered you. Even if you have been banished to the most distant land under the heavens, from there the Lord your God will gather you and bring you back. He will bring you to the land that belonged to your fathers, and you will take possession of it. (Deuteronomy 30:3-5; cf. Jeremiah 24:9; Hosea 9;17; Jeremiah 30:11)

These prophecies of a national return seem clear enough for anyone living in the twentieth century. But consider how difficult it might be for people to accept such prophecies prior to the twentieth century. Such prophecies were not as easy to appreciate for those living in the extremely long period before their fulfillment. How tempting it would be to "spiritualize" such prophecies and ignore their literal meaning.

But God predicted both that the Jews would be scattered throughout the nations and that He would return them to their land. These predictions occurred 2,600 years ago. As Dr. Henry Morris observes,

> That a nation could be completely destroyed as an organized entity by an invading army (as Israel was, by the Romans, in 70 A.D.), its people either slaughtered or scattered from one end of the

world to the other, its land occupied and ruled by aliens for 1900 years, and yet survived as a distinct nationality, and then finally regain its homeland and be recognized as a viable nation once more by the other nations of the world, seems impossible. Yet it has happened in spite of the impossibilities, and to make it still more amazing, it was predicted to happen many centuries before it happened. (Morris, p. 191)

The historical impossibility of a revived nation of Israel was why some Christians over the centuries concluded that God was through with Israel and that all the promises to her would therefore have to be fulfilled spiritually in the church and not literally to the nation.

Some people claim that the prophecies cited above were already fulfilled in history. For example, how do we know these prophecies do not refer to the Israelites returning after the Babylonian captivity? We can know this for several reasons.

First, when God spoke of the return from Babylon it was identified as such—as a return from Babylon. The Jews returned from Babylon specifically—not from all the nations of the world (Jeremiah 25:9-12; 29:10; Ezra 1:1-8). In other words, the Babylonian return could not involve an international regathering as the prophecies demand. But as we saw, God predicted an international return to Israel of people gathered from geographical areas other than Babylon.

Second, the prophecies reveal details that require they be placed after the Babylonian return and even after A.D. 70 or A.D. 1948 (Ezekiel 36:12-15, 24-38; 37:11-14, 21-28; chapters 38-39). When the Jews returned to Jerusalem under Nehemiah, they were never ruled by the predicted King, nor was their nation united in the manner predicted in Ezekiel 37:21-28.

Today, we are only seeing the beginning of the regathering of Israel. There is currently a regathering of the nation, but not in spiritual belief. However, a spiritual revival is promised to those who have gathered. But now let us recognize the amazing fact that these ancient prophecies have begun to be fulfilled.

Do the Ancient Prophecies Fit the Modern Facts?

No one can deny that these ancient prophecies have recently begun to be fulfilled. After the British-sponsored Balfour Declaration of 1917, international policy favored the Jews returning to their homeland. Although they initially returned in small numbers, by the time of the 1948 War of Independence, Jewish people began returning in the millions, a process that continues to this day. According to *Time* (January 14, 1991), by 1992, "nearly 1/3 of the estimated 3.5 million Jews remaining in the Soviet Union are expected in Israel." In several years, Israel expects an additional million immigrants from Russia and other countries.

Commenting on Ezekiel 38, Arnold Fruchtenbaum reveals that

> Israel is a land being brought back from the sword (38:8). After 1900 years, 46 invasions, the War of Independence, the land is Jewish again and free from foreign dominion. This nation is gathered from many nations and peoples (38:8, 12). The Jews in Israel today come from 80-90 different nations. The continual waste places are now inhabited (38:8, 12). The Israelis today are rebuilding the ancient places and turning them into modern towns and cities. They dwell securely (38:11, 14). This has often been misconstrued as meaning a state of peace. But this is not the meaning of the Hebrew root *batach*. The nominal form of this root means "security." This is not the security due to a state of peace, but security due to confidence in their own strength. This, too, is a good description of Israel today. The Israeli army has fought four wars since its founding and won them swiftly each time. Today, Israel is secure, confident that her army can repel any invasion from the Arab states. Hence, Israel is dwelling securely. Israel is dwelling in unwalled villages (38:11). This is very descriptive of the present day kibbutzim in Israel. (Fruchtenbaum, p. 80)

Because Israel is now a nation united once again as the Bible predicted, the other specific prophecies that were predicted for Israel in the Old Testament are now in line to be fulfilled.

16

The Amazing Fact: Israel Remains at Center Stage in World Politics

Many peoples and the inhabitants of many cities will yet come. . . . And many peoples and powerful nations will come to Jerusalem to seek the Lord Almighty and to entreat him.

Zechariah 8:20, 22
Cf. Payne, pp. 456, 657

What Are the Ancient Biblical Prophecies?

Zechariah 12:2-3 (520 B.C.):

I am going to make Jerusalem *a cup that sends all the surrounding peoples reeling.* Judah will be besieged as well as Jerusalem. On that day, when *all the nations of the earth* are gathered against her, I will make Jerusalem an immovable rock for all the nations. All who try to move it will injure themselves.

Jeremiah 3:14-15, 17 (600 B.C.):

"Return, faithless people," declares the Lord, "for I am your husband. I will choose you—one from a town and two from a clan—and bring you to Zion. Then I will give you shepherds after my own heart, who will lead you with knowledge and understanding. . . . At that time they will call Jerusalem The Throne, and *all nations will gather in Jerusalem* to honor the name of the Lord. No longer will they follow the stubbornness of their evil hearts.

Zechariah 14:16-17 (520 B.C.):

Then the survivors from all the nations that have attacked Jerusalem will go up year after year to worship the King, the Lord Almighty, and to celebrate the Feast of Tabernacles. If any of the peoples of the earth do not go up to Jerusalem to worship the King, the Lord Almighty, they will have no rain.

Isaiah 14:2 (700 B.C.):

Nations will take them and bring them to their own place. And *the house of Israel will possess the nations* as menservants and maidservants in the Lord's land. They will make captives of their captors and rule over their oppressors.

Isaiah 60:12, 15-16, 18-22 (700 B.C.; see Isaiah 49:23: 54:3):

For the nation or kingdom that will not serve you will perish; it will be utterly ruined. . . . Although you have been forsaken and hated, with no one traveling through, *I will make you the everlasting pride and joy of all generations.* You will drink the milk of nations and be nursed at royal breasts. Then you will know that I, the Lord, am your Savior. . . . No longer will violence be heard in your land, nor ruin or destruction within your borders. . . . The sun will no more be your light by day, nor will the brightness of the moon shine on you, for the Lord will be your everlasting light, and your God will be your glory. Your sun will never set again, and your moon will wane no more; the Lord will be your everlasting light, and your days of sorrow will end. Then will all your people be righteous and *they will possess the land forever.* They are the shoot I have planted, the work of my hands, for the display of my splendor. The least of you will become a thousand, the smallest a mighty nation. I am the Lord; *in its time I will do this swiftly.*

Do the Ancient Prophecies Fit the Modern Facts?

These prophecies predict that Israel will become the geographical focal point of all nations of the earth:

Who would have dreamed a century ago—or even 50 years ago—that this insignificant piece of real estate, after the Jews had returned to it, would be the focus of the world's attention week after week, year after year, decade after decade? And not casual or ordinary attention, but fear of how to deal with this new nation in relation to its Arab neighbors, and of how to prevent war in that area from becoming a global holocaust. Yet what has happened is exactly what the Bible prophesied: "Behold, I will make Jerusalem a cup of trembling unto all the people round about. . . ." (Zechariah 12:2).

And who would have been so foolish as to imagine that after Israel's rebirth this Lilliputian nation's armed forces would rival in power and exceed in efficiency those of the United States and Russia. Tiny Israel, occupying about one-sixth of one percent of the land in the Arab world, has been more than a match for the surrounding Arab nations, though they outnumber her about 40 to 1 and have been given every possible help from the Soviets, from the latest arms to technical and strategic advisors by the thousands. (Hunt, *Global*, p. 33)

Israel has become the center of the world's attention. Even now world events seem to be set in motion for Israel to increasingly dominate the news. In brief, what is happening in Israel today is a foreshadowing of what is to take place in greater detail in the future.

Now we will turn our attention to specific facts indicating that the world stage is being set for Israel to affect the destiny of the world. The subjects we discuss will include (1) the Palestinian problem, (2) the desire of the Arab nations to see Israel destroyed, (3) the increasing hostility of the world community toward the nation of Israel, and (4) growing worldwide anti-Semitism. These five facts will show that what the Bible foresees for Israel in the future is indeed plausible.

Israeli Refusal to Give Up the Occupied Territories and the Increasing Call for a Resolution to the Palestinian Issue

In the famous Six Day War of 1967, Israel regained control of Old Jerusalem, the West Bank, the Gaza Strip, the Golan Heights, and the Sinai Desert, which they later returned as part of a peace settlement with Egypt. Israel has no intention of giving away any other part of this hard-won territory.

Apart from a comprehensive, genuine peace settlement with its hostile Arab neighbors, Israel believes it would be foolish to give up the occupied lands, which are militarily strategic, providing a legitimate "buffer zone" of protection against constant terrorist attacks. In fact, the Bible predicts that at some future point Israel will again possess its ancient boundaries—and more. That means that much more territory, land now occupied by militant Arab nations, will someday belong to Israel (Genesis 15:18-21; cf. Genesis 17:8; Joshua 1:4). This includes most of Lebanon and Syria and half of Iraq and Jordan. All this territory is destined to fall into Jewish hands. At some future point, Israel will occupy more than ten times the land mass she now inhabits. But Muslim law will never permit this to occur without a holy war (Lindsey, p. 6). Thus, additional wars in the Middle East may be inevitable.

The current Palestinian problem is principally a fight over land and is only one of numerous issues dividing Jews and Arabs. The intractable nature of these problems in the Middle

East could easily play into the hands of the future world dictator the Bible calls the Antichrist (discussed in chapter 14).

The Bible predicts that this new political statesman will eventually rule the world. This leader will make a peace treaty agreed to and signed by Israel. But in spite of the agreement, this powerful politician will go back on his treaty and betray Israel (Daniel 9:27; 11:35-46). Commenting on this amazing prediction found in Daniel 9:27, Dr. Fruchtenbaum observes,

> This verse speaks of an individual making a seven year covenant with the Jewish nation. The Hebrew text emphasizes that this will be a firm and strong covenant . . . between Israel and the Antichrist which the Antichrist will break halfway through. . . . The covenant is made with many, but not with all. The Hebrew text has a definite article and so a more correct translation would be the many. The many who make this covenant will have to include the leaders of Israel empowered to sign covenants of this nature. (Fruchtenbaum, pp. 131-32)

Today, as we soberly contemplate the dangerous potential of the Middle East, the prophetic scenario points us in a frightening direction. Political and other realities are so intractable and complex that it is plausible now to believe that a future world leader like the Antichrist will come forth to present a brilliant peace plan that would be acceptable to the nations involved. News commentator Tom Brokaw, referring to the 1991 Gulf War in the Middle East and the geopolitical/military complexities (including the possibility of future wars), noted that the entire situation "is ever more complicated than even the worst case scenarios contemplated" (February 21, 1991, NBC News).

At this moment, if the whole world is unable to resolve the Middle East dilemma, doesn't this suggest that the stage is now set for a political leader to step forth with a plan? Fact number one, then, is Israel's refusal to give up its land. That will cause constant friction that will allow for a powerful world ruler to emerge with a brilliant plan to bring peace to the area.

Most Arab Nations Desire the Complete Destruction of Israel

Practically speaking, a comprehensive Jewish-Arab peace is thought by many to be virtually impossible. It is true that Israel may make certain concessions/treaties with certain Arab/Muslim states in the future. It may even sign a U.S.-Israel "guarantee of peace" treaty. But while there are several options in the near future, the prophecies predict that the end result will be a different story.

In 1964, the PLO was formed with the express purpose of destroying Israel and making a Palestinian state where Israel once resided. The vast majority of Arab nations have agreed in the past with the goals of the PLO. But whatever happens with the PLO, there is another potential powder keg called Jihad, or holy war.

Thus, one ingredient complicating things in this complex political region is the increasingly militant fundamentalist Islamic groups that propose Jihad, such as the one calling itself "Islamic Jihad." These Islamic groups cite the Koran in support of their goals.

As one television documentary observed, "Arabs and Jews are locked in a struggle to the death"; Islam and Judaism are on a collision course. It further noted that Jihad and martyrdom "are inscribed in the heart of Islam" and are considered a holy means of achieving Islamic objectives, so that every piece of land in the Middle East must become Muslim ("Terror").

Organizations such as Islamic Jihad intend to bring Islamic law to Palestine (Israel), and terror is the preferred means to accomplish the goal. Thus, radical Islamic groups such as Islamic Jihad are living by a philosophy of violence ("Terror").

This hatred between Jews and Arabs appears almost intractable. It seems peace cannot be made without crossing a river of blood. How did this Arab-Jewish conflict begin? It started when a division occurred between Abraham's sons—Isaac, the son God promised Abraham, and Ishmael, the son born out of impatience with waiting for God's promise.

Isaac became the father of the Jews; Ishmael became the father of the Arabs (Genesis 16:11-12; Galatians 4:28-29; Psalm 83:4-6). The results of this emotional conflict between the descendants of the two sons of Abraham is described in award-winning writer George Grant's *The Blood of the Moon*. He begins by discussing the importance of the Islamic holy war:

> According to Islamic tradition, the complete military subjugation of the earth is mandated by Allah. . . . In the *Hadith*, Mohammed said: "Hear, O *Muslims*, the meaning of life. Shall I not tell you of the peak of the matter, its pillar, and its topmost part? The peak of the matter is Islam itself. The pillar is ritual *Rakatin*—prayer. And the topmost part is *Ji' had*—holy war. (Grant, p. 41)

Next, Grant shows that the Koran itself is anti-Jewish. Consider the following citations giving Allah's instruction.

> You shall surely find the most violent of all men in enmity against the Umma [Muslims] to be the Jews. ([Sura] 5:82)

> O, true believers, take not the Jews and the Christians for your friends. They cannot be trusted. They are defiled—filth. (Lindsey, *Earth*, p. 51)

> The Jews are smitten with vileness and misery and drew on themselves indignation from Allah. (Tan, *Prophecy*, p. 61)

> Wherever they are found, the Jews reek of destruction—which is their just reward. (Fruchtenbaum, p. 112)

Grant further shows that,

> according to the Meccan chronicles of that early period, recorded in the *Sahih Moslem* annals, all Jews were anathema and were to be annihilated: "Allah's messenger—may peace be upon him—has commanded: Fight against the Jews and kill them. Pursue them until even a stone would say: "Come here Moslem, there is a Jew hiding himself behind me. Kill him. Kill him quickly." (Grant, pp. 48-49)

The hostility of the Arabs against the Jews can also be seen in reading the numerous statements by Arab leaders during the 1948 independence of Israel:

> The day after Israel officially became a nation on May 14, 1948, three Palestinian Arab armies . . . launched a bitter war for control of the entire Palestinian region. According to the Arab leaders, there was absolutely no possibility for any sort of compromise or negotiated peace. Haj Amin el Husseini, the *Mufti* of Jerusalem . . . who now led the Palestinian Arab resistance, declared: "The entire Jewish population in Palestine must be destroyed or be driven into the sea; Allah has bestowed upon us the rare privilege of finishing what Hitler only began. Let the *Ji'had* begin. Murder the Jews. Murder them all."
>
> King Abdul Aziz Ibn Saud, the founding monarch of the Saudi sultanate, said: "The Arab nations should sacrifice up to ten million of their fifty million people, if necessary, to wipe out Israel. Israel to the Arab world is like a cancer to the human body. And the only way of remedy is to uproot it."
>
> Azzam Pasha, secretary general of the Arab League, asserted that: "This will be a war of extermination and a momentous massacre which will be spoken of like the Mongolian massacres and the Crusades. No Jew will be left alive."
>
> King Farouk of Egypt concurred: "The Jews in Palestine must be exterminated. There can be no other option for those of us who revere the name of Allah. There will be no *Dhimma*. There will only be *Ji'had*."
>
> From King Abdullah of Trans-Jordon to Zahir Shah of Afghanistan, from Imam Yahya of Yemen to King Hussan of Morocco, from Reza Shah of Iran to Regent Abd al Ilah of Iraq, every Moslem leader in the Middle East called for the destruction of Israel and the execution of the Jews. Even the moderate King Idris of Libya sounded the call for genocide: ". . . There can be no compromise until every Jew is dead and gone." (Grant, pp. 52-54)

But today, as everyone is only too aware, little has changed. Consider the following illustration:

Violence and strife have become a regular part of the Palestine landscape—as familiar as the Judean hills. And still, the hatred is unabated.

Sheikh Tamimi, the current *Mufti* of Jerusalem who was responsible for organizing the ill-fated [1990] Temple Mount uprising, recently issued a call for all Moslems to join arms against Israel. "The Jews are destined to be persecuted, humiliated, and tortured forever, and it is a Moslem duty to see to it that they reap their due. No petty arguments must allowed to divide us. Where Hitler failed we must succeed."

Yasser Arafat, the longtime chairman of the PLO and the mastermind behind the Intifada uprising in the West Bank and Gaza Strip, has said again and again: . . . "The Jews must be removed and Israel must be annihilated. We can accept nothing less."

Hafez al Assad of Syria agreed: "We shall never call for nor accept peace. We shall only accept war. We have resolved to drench this land with Israel's blood, to oust the Jews as aggressors, and to throw them all into the sea.". . .

As a result of this intractable conflict, every problem in the Middle East is now somehow connected to the Palestinian question. For instance, when Saddam Hussein overran Kuwait in 1990, he blamed the conflict on Israel. Likewise, when Hafez al Assad completed his conquest of Lebanon that same year, he blamed the crisis on Israel. When Muammar Qaddafi of Libya sparked a coup in Chad, also in 1990, he blamed the situation on Israel. This seemingly absurd linkage has become inescapable.

As Hashemi Rafsanjani of Iran explained: "Every problem in our region can be traced to this single dilemma: the occupation of *Dar al Islam* by Jewish infidels or Western imperialists. Every political controversy, every boundary dispute, and every internal conflict is spawned by the inability of the *Umma* [Muslim] to faithfully and successfully wage *Ji' had*. The everlasting struggle between Ishmael and Isaac cannot cease until one or the other is utterly vanquished." (Grant, pp. 55-56)

The Arab/Muslim hostility against Israel makes the biblical prophecies all the more relevant. There is little hope for a genuine and lasting peace in the Middle East. Being only too aware of how the Arab nations feel toward them, Israel is reluctant to negotiate any peace treaty imposed on them from the West.

Increasing World Hostility Toward Israel

After the recent war in the Gulf, the world has never felt more favorable toward Israel. Why is the world so friendly toward Israel? First, even after forty SCUD missile attacks, Israel expressed Herculean restraint and never responded militarily. This has led to a good feeling about Israel and to the reduction of the political power of the radical Palestinian movement.

But this situation must change. Why? We all know that the U.S. coalition against Iraq was based on a dozen United Nations resolutions that everyone agreed were fair and just. But in another category the U.N. has voted on what it considers "fair" and "just"—the establishment of a Palestinian homeland. So the questions is, Will the U.N. attempt to force Israel to give back the land that they took from the Arabs? Both President Bush and the world have said Israel must exchange land for peace.

But we have just seen how difficult this will be for Israel to accept. Whatever happens in the short term, all this good will toward Israel will eventually be whittled away. If the U.S. can wage war on Iraq for annexing Kuwait, the Arab world will want to know why the U.S. shouldn't bring pressure to bear against Israel to force them to give back the land they took in war. Israel will thus remain between a rock and hard place in spite of any temporary good feelings many now have toward Israel.

We have said that biblical prophecy envisions Israel at center stage. Few would deny that an intractable Israeli position on its occupied territories would only increase the animosity of the nations toward Israel. Why? The Western world survives on Arab oil. The Arabs who control that oil hate Israel. Who would deny that the world's approach to Israel could easily become regulated by its vital dependence on oil?

Meanwhile, Israel faces great opposition and testing. The Arab oil pressure has political objectives. This is evidenced by the main

UN General Assembly resolution concerning Israel: "Zionism [the creation of a home in Palestine for Jewish people, secured by public law] is a form of racism and racial discrimination." Not long ago, Carl Rowan commented that seventy-two countries were openly hostile to Israel, with thirty-two others tottering on the fence.

Such events raise crucial questions. Is the Israel we know today the Israel that will be ringed by foes at the end of the age? Are we beginning to see the pressures that will issue in the great prophetic events to come—in the time of Jacob's trouble [Armageddon] and the divine deliverance of God's people? We can only wait and see. One thing is clear: The eyes of the world are turning toward a strategic portion of our globe, the point where Africa, Europe, and Asia intersect, and the place the Bible tells us will be the focus of end-time events. (James, *Arabs*, pp. 72-73)

Anyone who studies the U.N. resolutions relating to Israel cannot deny that the world community considers Israel something of a thorn in the flesh.

Anti-Semitism Is Growing Worldwide

Part of the reason for this animosity toward Jewish people can be seen in the book of Revelation. Here we discover that Satan himself has a special hatred for the Jews. Thus, many of the horrors and tragedies experienced by the Jews throughout history are to some extent a result of satanically induced persecution. As Hal Lindsey comments concerning Revelation 12,

The woman (Israel) is hated and persecuted by *the dragon* (Satan 12:9) because she gives birth to *a Son* (the Messiah) *who is to rule all the nations* (12:1-6). Satan hates Israel with an undying passion because she is the instrument through which the Messiah, His conqueror, was born. Satan also hates Israel because God's reality and veracity are proven by the way He has kept the many prophecies and promises He made to Israel, even though she hasn't deserved it. These amazing fulfillments are recorded in history for all honest inquirers to see. (Lindsey, *Road*, p. 5)

But satanically induced persecution is not the only reason for Israel's difficulties.

Throughout her history, Israel has often disobeyed her divine calling and pursued false gods and evil practices, bringing God's chastisement. The judgment of God upon Israel for this disobedience is also recorded in history. These judgments are painfully listed in Leviticus 26 and Deuteronomy 28. "But if you will not listen to me and carry out all these commands, and if you reject my decrees and abhor my laws and fail to carry out all my commands and so violate my covenant, then I will do this to you: I will bring upon you sudden terror" (Leviticus 26:14-16).

Nevertheless, in spite of God's promises to chastise Israel for her sins, He also promised Abraham that He would make an unconditional covenant with his descendants—the nation of Israel. In spite of their sins, He would be faithful to His promise to bless them, and through them all the nations (Genesis 12:2). This promise is repeated throughout the Bible.*

But God promised something else—that the nations that cursed Israel would be cursed by Him: "I will bless those who bless you, and whoever curses you I will curse" (Genesis 12:3; cf., 15:5; 18:18; 22:18; 26:4; 27:29; 28:4, 14; Exodus 23:22; Numbers 24:9; Deuteronomy 9:5; 30:7; Psalm 72:17; Isaiah 19:25; Acts 3:25; Galatians 3:8). What the nations who currently persecute Israel do not understand is that God Himself will bring judgment on these very nations. The prophets warned, "Whoever touches you [Israel] touches the apple of his eye"(Zechariah 2:8).

---

*Genesis 13:16; 15:5; 17:2, 4; 18:18; 22:17, 18; 26:4; 28:3, 14; 32:12; 35:11; 41:49; 46:3; 47:27; 48:4, 16, 19; Exodus 1:7; 5:5; 32:13; Deuteronomy 1:10; 10:22; 13:17; 26:5; Joshua 11:4; 24:3; 2 Samuel 17:11; 1 Kings 3:8; 4:20; 1 Chronicles 27:23; 2 Chronicles 1:9; Nehemiah 9:23; Psalm 107:38; Isaiah 6:13; 10:22; 19:24; 48:19; 51:2; 54:3; 60:22; Jeremiah 4:2; 33:22; Micah 4:7; Haggai 2:9; Zechariah 8:13; Malachi 3:2; Isaiah 19:24; 44:3; 61:9; 65:23; Genesis 24:1, 35; 25:1; 26:3; 28:4; Exodus 20:24; Numbers 22:12; 23:8, 20; 24:9; Psalm 67:6; 115:12.

Thus, "The Lord your God will put all these curses on your enemies who hate and persecute you" (Deuteronomy 30:7).

The history of the nation of Israel is indeed unlike that of any other nation throughout human history. No other nation has been so blessed by God and yet so hated by Satan. The factors of satanic persecution, divine judgment for sin, and divine blessing honoring the promises to Abraham are all evident throughout Jewish history. Only these realities can explain the current situation Israel finds herself in (Hunt, *CIB*).

Initially, Israel was more than willing to share Palestine with the Arabs. The Israelis encouraged the Arabs to remain in Palestine, but Arab leaders would not have it.

> Contrary to reports that they drove Arabs from their homes, the Jews tried to persuade them to remain. For example, in April, 1948, the British chief of police in Haifa, A. J. Bridmead, reported: "Every effort is being made by the Jews to persuade the Arab population to remain." A foreign visitor reported, "In Tiberias I saw a placard affixed to a sealed Arab mosque that read: 'We did not dispossess them . . . [and] the day will come when the Arabs will return to their homes and property in this town. In the meantime let no citizen touch their property. Signed, Jewish Town Council of Tiberias.'"
>
> The London Economist (Oct. 2, 1948) declared: "The Israeli authorities urged all Arabs to remain . . . [but] the announcement [was] made over the air by the Arab Higher Executive urging all Arabs to leave . . . [because] upon the final withdrawal of the British the combined armies of the Arab states would invade Palestine and drive the Jews into the sea." The Jordan daily, Al Difaa, complained on 9-6-48: "The Arab governments told us, 'Get out so that we can get in.' So we got out, but they did not get in." (Hunt, *CIB*)

Even *Time* magazine of April 4, 1988, commented, "Had Egypt, Syria and other Arabs nations accepted Israel's right to exist in 1947, the Palestinians could have been living for the past 40 years in a state of their own." But the Arabs hated the Jews so fervently that they brought massive dislocation and hardship to the Palestinians. Arab intransigence and irrational hatred of the Jews has thus caused far more death and destruction to Arabs than Israel has ever done or ever wanted to do. For example, in a single Palestinian uprising against Jordan in 1970 far more Palestinians were killed than by Israel in its entire forty-three-year history. In 1967, when Israel took the West Bank for reasons of self-defense, it also offered to give the land back if the Arabs would simply recognize Israel's right to exist. The uniform Arab response was, "No recognition of Israel, no negotiation, and no peace" (Hunt, *CIB*).

Nor has the PLO democratically represented the Palestinians. The PLO was not founded by the Palestinians. It was founded by Egypt's President Nasser. The current leader of PLO, Yasser Arafat, was not voted president by the Palestinians but by the PLO Central Committee.

Arafat is the nephew of Haj Amin el' Husseini, the past grand Mufti of Jerusalem, an admirer of Hitler. Haj Amin has publicly acknowledged that the Arabs supported the Axis powers in World War II because they promised a final solution to "the Jewish problem." The Nazi and Arab leaders were in agreement concerning the extermination of the world's Jews (Hunt, *CIB*).

Statements that reflect Nazi Germany's hatred against the Jews are today, quite literally, "being screamed by Muslim leaders in mosques everywhere!" Thus, "The Satanic spirit that inspired Hitler's Holocaust continues to call for 'peace,' and demands the same price. Yasser Arafat sees the extermination of the Jews as a sacred Islamic duty of the PLO, whose very charter calls for Israel's destruction" (Hunt, *CIB*).

> Islam nurtures the hatred that creates a Saddam Hussein, an Arafat or Egypt's Nasser, who also used poison gas in his war against Yemen. When Kaddafi roars, "The battle with Israel must be such that after it, Israel will cease to exist," he cannot be dismissed as lacking Islamic compassion. Such Hitlerian threats pour continuously from the mouths of Muslim religious and political leaders over radios and loudspeakers and TV in every Arab country.

The Islamic world is one of constant unrest, double-cross, uprisings and wars. Arab leaders distrust one another and fight among themselves. Only Islam and the passion to destroy Israel unites them. Yet Islam itself has inspired this way of life.

Kuwait was the chief paymaster to the PLO and its international terrorists, who "fight Israel" by killing civilians. After a number of diplomats, including a U.S. Ambassador, were killed by terrorists, the Emir of Kuwait was asked whether he would continue to finance the PLO. He replied that he would indeed, "with unlimited funds." The PLO repaid that kindness by giving intelligence data to Iraq for its invasion of Kuwait—after which Arafat declared: "We say to the brother and leader Saddam Hussein, 'Go forward with God's [Allah's] blessing!'" Behold a brotherhood of murderers!

Saudi Arabia's fulminations against Israel have been no less extreme than Saddam's or Arafat's. Typical has been the following from Saudi King Fahd: "The media must urge the Muslims to launch *Jihad* [holy war] . . . united in the confrontation with the Jews and those who support them." That Kuwait and Saudi Arabia had to turn to "infidels" and "Israel supporters" to rescue them from an admired Islamic leader bent upon their destruction must affect the thinking in the entire Arab world. Yet hatred for Israel will remain.

A renewed wave of anti-semitism is sweeping the world. For example, in Poland, Jewish cemeteries are once again being defaced with swastikas. . . . Warsaw's Jewish State Theatre has been defaced with slogans such as, "Jews to the ovens." Poland's new president, Lech Walesa, a Catholic, declared on TV: "A gang of Jews took over our resources and exploited our land, and their aim is to destroy us." Hitler said the same.

After Kuwait's rape, Jerusalem's Catholic patriarch, Michel Sabbah, commended Saddam for "truly carry[ing] in his heart the Palestinian cause," and would not concede that Saddam was "more dangerous" than President Bush. Iraq's ranking Catholic leader, Patriarch Raphael Bidawid, defended Saddam's invasion and annexation of Kuwait and its missile attacks upon Israel's civilians. "This entire war has been planned by Israel," said Bidawid from Rome, where he was conferring with the Pope and other Vatican officials about Middle East "peace." The Roman

Catholic Church, which opposes Jewish control of Jerusalem, has yet to acknowledge Israel's right to exist in the 43 years since it became a state. (Hunt, *CIB*)

But sadly, the modern situation encouraging anti-Semitism has historic antecedents even in the church. In *The Road to Holocaust*, Hal Lindsey shows how anti-Semitism can be encouraged in the church through a particular interpretation of Bible prophecy that began with Origen and Augustine and has remained to this day. While not necessarily agreeing with all of Lindsey's analysis, we do accept the premise that a nonliteral interpretation of prophecy as practiced in the church historically can, under the right circumstances, become one plank in the platform of anti-Semitism. And this, of course, can make the entire issue of how one interprets prophetic Scripture of vital importance.

This particular interpretation sees the nation of Israel as rejected and cursed by God; the church has replaced Israel and become the recipient of all its ancient promises. "From this error in eschatology . . . to outright anti-Semitism was only a matter of time" (Lindsey, *Road*, p. 9).

Thus, once the Christian church abandoned the literal interpretation of prophecy and the logical outcome, premillennialism, it could discard all evidence of God's divine plan for and protection of Israel.

Lindsey details the horrors perpetrated by the church against Jews during the Middle Ages and particularly the Crusades. He shows that one underlying factor in this persecution was the church's rejection of a literal interpretation of prophecy (Lindsey, *Road*, p. 17).

Thus, when anti-Semitism is encouraged today, even in veiled forms, the church must be careful to guard against repeating the errors of the past. God Himself clearly warns against mistreatment of the Jews. In Romans 11, he warns the church that Israel remains the "holy" and "elect" of God and is indeed "loved" by God because "God's gifts and his call are irrevocable" (Romans 11:29). He warns that the church should not be boastful against the Jews—as if the church stands solely on its own power. In fact, it is the promises to the Jews that support the church (Romans 11:18).

Therefore, the church should confess God's commitment to Israel and fear the consequences of arrogantly rejecting that association (v. 17-21). Thus,

> a false theological climate can breed anti-Semitism like a plague. Even good people are not immune to these kinds of lies, because the master deceiver, that father of lies, Satan himself, is behind it. This is why the Church must not allow this kind of climate to develop again." (Lindsey, *Road*, p. 19)

Many people think that Christians are immune from anti-Semitism. But no one is immune. Even the great reformer, theologian, and biblical expositor Martin Luther succumbed to anti-Semitism in his later years. For example, he wrote a tract in 1543 that would have been indistinguishable from anything produced by Nazi Germany. After quoting this tract, Lindsey rightly comments:

> Is it any wonder that Hitler and [Nazi] Julius Streicher quoted Martin Luther as justification for their murderous "Final Solution for the Jews?"
>
> The fact that such a great man of faith and the Scriptures as Luther could be seduced by Satan to write such a monstrous thing proves two things: First, the anti-Jewish propaganda within the Church and society in general was virulently latent and thoroughly embedded in the culture. Second, the original false interpretation of prophecy, which Luther retained from Augustine, was a powerful blinding force that kept even the great reformer, who was an otherwise brilliant and literal interpreter of the Scriptures, from grasping what God's Word literally and unconditionally taught: that the Jews are still His elect people with a definite future in His plan. It also kept him from seeing an oft repeated Biblical lesson: That even though God Himself disciplines Israel, woe to the man or nation who mistreats them. History is strewn with the wreckage of former great leaders and nations who treated the Israelites unjustly. (Lindsey, *Road*, p. 24)

That is why the situation in the modern Middle East is so hazardous. Scores of nations oppose Israel and are ultimately courting divine judgment.

In conclusion, Lindsey argues that the manner in which many of the later church Fathers had allegorically interpreted biblical prophecy (concerning Israel and its future) resulted historically in incredible but unnecessary suffering for the Jews. His reason for writing *The Road to Holocaust* was his concern that we are now witnessing a revival of the same false interpretations of prophecy that in the past led to such tragedy. An example of the attitude engendered by the modern reconstructionist/dominionist interpretation of Bible prophecy is illustrated in one reconstructionist's recent message:

> The Kingdom has been taken over from Israel, and it has been possessed by the New Covenant People. Israel has become demon possessed. It has become a nation of false prophets. A nation in the image of a Pagan Roman state. Jerusalem has become a harlot. And is going to be excommunicated. And the covenant promises are inherited by the faithful, witnessing, ruling Church of royal priests. That's what [the book of] Revelation is all about. (Lindsey, *Road*, p. 25)

Lindsey comments:

> This is the same sort of rhetoric that in the past formed the basis of contempt for the Jews that later developed into outright anti-Semitism. . . . Let Christians not sit idly by while a system of prophetic interpretation that historically furnished the philosophical basis for anti-Semitism infects the Church again. (Lindsey, *Road*, p. 25)

17

Will Christ Rescue Christians from Earth in a Dramatic Rapture?

All miracles are simply feeble lights like beacons on our way
to the port where shines the light, the total light of the
resurrection.

Jacques Ellul

The Incarnation is the most stupendous event which ever can
take place on earth; and after it and henceforth, I do not see
how we can scruple at any miracle on the mere ground of it
being unlikely to happen.

John Henry Newman

What Are the Ancient Prophecies?

1 Thessalonians 4:15-18 (A.D. 50):

> According to the Lord's own word, we tell you that we who are
> still alive, who are left till the coming of the Lord, will certainly
> not precede those who have fallen asleep. *For the Lord himself
> will come down from heaven,* with a loud command, with the
> voice of the archangel and with the trumpet call of God, and the
> dead in Christ will rise first. After that, *we who are still alive and*

are left will be caught up together with them in the clouds to meet the Lord in the air. And so we will be with the Lord forever. Therefore, encourage each other with these words.

Matthew 24:41 (ca. A.D. 50):

Two men will be in the field: *one will be taken* and the other left. Two women will be grinding with a handmill; *one will be taken* and the other left.

1 Corinthians 15:50-53 (A.D. 55):

I declare to you, brothers, that flesh and blood cannot inherit the kingdom of God, nor does the perishable inherit the imperishable. Listen, I tell you a mystery: We will not all sleep, but we will all be changed—in a flash, in the twinkling of an eye, at the last trumpet. For the trumpet will sound, the dead will be raised imperishable and *we will be changed.* For the perishable must clothe itself with the imperishable, and the mortal with immortality.

Scholars have picked a Latin word that summarizes the event described in 1 Thessalonians 4:15-18 and other verses. The Latin word they chose is *rapio,* meaning "caught up," from which we get our English word "rapture" (128:1523).

The historic meaning of the rapture has always referred to the imminent return of Christ in which He will remove all true believers from the earth and take them to be with Him. *Baker's Dictionary of Theology* comments on this term and its biblical significance:

Derived from the Latin *rapio,* "to seize," "to snatch," the word may . . . refer to a removal from one place to another by forcible means. . . . When they [the dead] are raised, the living saints will be "caught up" (*harpagesometha*) together with them in clouds to meet the Lord in the air. . . .

The verb *harpazo* occurs thirteen times in the NT. We read that the Spirit caught up Philip near Gaza and brought him to Caesarea (Acts 8:39). Paul was caught up into Paradise, where he experienced ineffable things (II Cor. 12:2-4). [The Two Witnesses were caught up to heaven in the sight of their enemies, Revelation 11:11-12] There can be no doubt that Paul's language in I Thess. 4:17 requires a removal of the saints from earth at the time of the Lord's return. (p. 433)

Jesus Himself promised, "And if I go and prepare a place for you, *I will come back and take you to be with me* that you also may be where I am" (John 14:3). In this verse and the verses cited above, it is clear what Jesus taught: (1) He promised to return for all true believers; (2) He Himself would descend from heaven; and (3) those who were alive at this point would be caught up—raptured—to meet Him in the air. In 1 Corinthians 15, where it talks about the dead being raised incorruptible, Paul states, "And we shall be changed." The "we" referred to here is the raptured believers. The "last trump" mentioned is the same trump of God found in 1 Thessalonians 4:16.

Thus, "we" the living, will be changed supernaturally. When Christ returns for His own, we will instantly put on immortality and receive resurrected bodies (1 Corinthians 15:35-49; Philippians 3:21).

All Christian scholars agree that there will be a rapture; however, there is a question concerning when the rapture will occur in relation to the Tribulation period. The Tribulation period is a seven-year span of time described in the book of Revelation (chapters 6-19) that involves the outpouring of God's wrath upon the world for its evil. The question raised over the rapture is whether it occurs *before* the Tribulation, at some point *during* the Tribulation or *after* the Tribulation. Why do we believe the rapture occurs *before* the Tribulation period?

The first reason is because this is the only way in which the church can avoid the wrath of God poured out upon the world during the Tribulation. This is suggested by various verses. In 1 Thessalonians 1:9-10, we are promised that Jesus "delivers us from the wrath to come." In 1 Thessalonians 5:9 the context of the phrase "God has not appointed us to wrath" indicates a pretribulation rapture. The word wrath here is used of God's general wrath against sin (Romans 1:18) and also of His wrath during the Great Tribulation (Revelation 6:17; 14:10, 19). If we are delivered from the wrath to come, this could refer to God's future wrath against sin as displayed in the Tribulation period.

The second reason we believe in the pretribulation rapture is found in 1 Thessalonians 4:18, where genuine comfort and consolation are promised for the believer. But if the church must first pass through the Tribulation, we wonder how believers can "encourage each other with these words" and receive "eternal encouragement and good hope [to] encourage your hearts and strengthen you in every good deed and word." How can Christians be so encouraged if they know they must first pass through the unparalleled horrors of the Great Tribulation? These things are stated in the context of Christ's coming for His people. This is why the fact of our encouragement and hope indicates a rapture before the Tribulation.

This same thought appears to be stated in Revelation 3:10, where believers are promised to be kept "from the hour of trial, that is going to come upon the whole world to test those who live on the earth." It is possible to interpret the Greek as meaning either (1) to be kept *from* that very hour or (2) being safe *during* this trial. But if the pretribulational rapture is established on an independent basis, the meaning would then be obvious that we are kept *from* the hour of trial itself (i.e., the Great Tribulation). The question then becomes, can we establish a pretribulation rapture on other grounds? We think we can (cf. Keil & Delitzsch).

The third reason we accept a pretribulation rapture is because of the doctrine of immanency. The doctrine of immanency is inseparably connected with the doctrine of pretribulationism. Why? Because if Christ can return at any moment, there is no *necessary* intervening event prior to that return. For Christ to return for His people at literally any moment demands that there are no world events that must take place before Christ can come. If He returned after the Tribulation or at some point during the Tribulation, then immanency could not be true. Why? Because then Christ could not return until after Tribulation events, and the Bible does not teach that (Matthew

24:36-41; 1 Thessalonians 5:2-3; Luke 12:39-40). Therefore, if Christ's coming for believers is imminent, then it must be before the terrible events prophesied to happen during the Tribulation. If it wasn't, Christ's rapture of the church would not take any Christians by surprise—"like a thief in the night."

That is exactly how Jesus described His coming—like that of a thief in the night:

> Therefore, keep watch, because you do not know on what day your Lord will come. But understand this: If the owner of the house had known at what time of night the thief was coming, he would have kept watch and would not have let his house be broken into. So you also must be ready, because the Son of Man will come at an hour when you do not expect Him. (Matthew 24:42-44)

Obviously, if someone knows when a thief will come, he will be ready for the thief to prevent him from stealing his possessions. What Jesus is teaching here is that we obviously do not know the time of His coming, since it is described like the actions of an undetected thief. If we did know the exact time, there would be no reason to watch and keep alert. If we do not know the exact time of His coming, and yet Jesus warns us to be ready, then the only conclusion is that His coming can occur at any moment.

Jesus also paralleled His return with the days of Noah:

> No one knows about that day or hour, not even the angels in heaven, nor the Son, but only the Father.* As it was in the days of Noah, so it will be at the Coming of the Son of Man. For in the days before the Flood, people were eating and drinking, marrying and giving in marriage, up to the day Noah entered the Ark; and they knew nothing about what would happen until the Flood came and took them all away. That is how it will be at the Coming of the Son of Man. Two

---

*Archbishop Trench, the noted Greek scholar translated Mark 13:32: "If I were not God, as well as man, even I should not know the day nor the hour" (Adler, p. 17). This translation denies that Jesus as God did not know when He would return.

men will be in the field; one will be taken and the other left. Two women will be grinding with a hand mill; one will be taken and the other left. Therefore, keep watch. (Matthew 24:36-42)

The Scripture clearly teaches that the return of Christ is imminent. Jesus Himself taught, "Be on guard! Be alert! You do not know when that time will come" (Mark 13:33). He also said, "Therefore, keep watch, because you do not know the day or the hour" (Matthew 25:13). Imminency, then, seems to demand the pretribulational view.

But there are other reasons to hold a pretribulational view of the rapture. Revelation 20:1-3 teaches that in a future time an angel of God will come and seize the devil and bind him for a thousand years. Revelation 20:4 also says that those who had been martyred for Christ "came to life and reigned with Christ a thousand years."

The first issue is: What is this thousand-year period? Is it a literal thousand years or merely a figurative expression for a long time? The context demands that we interpret these words as a literal thousand-year period of time. So this thousand years, called the Millennium, is the period of time that we start with.

The second issue is that Revelation 20:4 teaches that those who come to life *will reign with Christ*. If they reigned with Christ, obviously Christ is there already for Him to be reigning for a thousand years. Again, this demands a literal thousand year reign of Christ.

The third issue is that the thousand-year period of time could only have started when Christ arrived and began to reign. Obviously, then, Christ must have come at the beginning of that time period. This establishes a premillennial return of Jesus Christ.

The fourth issue is that, when Jesus returns to earth to start the Millennium, that is not the rapture spoken of in 1 Thessalonians 4. Why? The timing is wrong. In 2 Thessalonians 2:3 Paul says concerning Christ's return to earth that *it will not come* until the rebellion occurs and the man of lawlessness is revealed, the man doomed to destruction. In verse 8, it is Jesus' return that destroys the Antichrist. This passage indicates that when Jesus comes to earth and sets up his millennial kingdom, immediately preceding that time the Antichrist will be deceiving the world during the Tribulation period.

Now, this return after the Tribulation is different from the return of Christ in the air in 1 Thessalonians 4:16-17, which states,

> for the Lord Himself will come down from heaven with a loud command with the voice of the archangel and with the trumpet call of God and the dead in Christ will rise first. After that, we are still alive and are left *will be caught up together with them in the clouds to meet the Lord in the air.* And so we will be with the Lord forever.

In this return of Christ, there are several differences compared to the return of Christ described in 2 Thessalonians 2:1-8. First, in 2 Thessalonians, Jesus comes to earth to defeat and banish the Antichrist. Christ then sets up his millennial kingdom. But in 1 Thessalonians Christ does not come down to earth; rather believers are "caught up together . . . to meet the Lord in the air." This is the rapture.

Second, Paul says about this rapture of Christians who will meet Christ in the air, "For you know very well that the day of the Lord will come *like a thief in the night.* While people are saying *peace and safety*, destruction will come on them *suddenly* as labor pains on a pregnant women and they will not escape" (1 Thessalonians 5:2-3). Here, it is plain that the return of Christ comes suddenly and by surprise. But this unexpected surprise return of Christ cannot be what is described in 2 Thessalonians 2:1-8, where His return *cannot happen* until the rebellion occurs, the Antichrist comes, and the Tribulation takes place.

Third, 1 Thessalonians 5 describes people imagining themselves in "peace and safety." They certainly wouldn't be saying that if the circumstances described in 2 Thessalonians were taking place, namely the Antichrist bringing the entire world more misery and destruction than it has ever before experienced (Matthew 24:15, 21).

Fourth, in 1 Thessalonians 4:18, the apostle Paul admonishes us: "Therefore encourage each other with these words." The encouragement in these words stems from the fact that it teaches that Christians are going to be spared the Great Tribulation as a result of being caught up to meet the Lord in the air. That would indeed be an encouragement to Christians. It is clearly more comforting to escape the Great Tribulation than to live through its horrors.

These four points place the rapture before the Tribulation. So the logical sequence from the Scriptures seems to be (1) the pretribulational rapture of the church followed by (2) the Antichrist and Tribulation period itself followed by (3) the return of Christ to earth (with the saints) to (4) establish His millennial kingdom, which will last a thousand years. In sorting out what the Bible teaches concerning end times, it is important to distinguish (1) Jews, (2) the believing church, and (3) the unbelieving Gentiles or pagans. These three categories of humanity must be distinguished to interpret prophecy properly.

For example, consider the Jews. The Old Testament prophecies concerning Israel will not be fulfilled by the church. Nor will they be fulfilled by the Gentiles from which Israel was separated as a nation. The prophecies remain to be fulfilled in the nation of Israel itself. This is the normal conclusion one arrives at when interpreting Old Testament prophecy literally. Thus, Israel is not part of the church:

> As surely as Gentiles continue to exist outside the church, so does Israel, with all of God's promises and plans for her remaining in full force. In fact, most "last days" prophecies are concerned with Israel, for she will continue here upon earth to face the Antichrist and the "time of Jacob's trouble" (Jeremiah 30:7) after the church has been raptured to heaven. As for the church, God's plans for her are unique and different from His plans for either Israel or the Gentile nations. (Hunt, *Global*, p. 28)

Consider the church. After the death of Christ on the cross, a new entity distinct from Jew and Gentile was born—the church. Jesus promised that He would build His church and that the gates of hell would not prevail against it (Matthew 16:18). The church is a unique spiritual organism that is distinct from the categories of Jew and Gentile even though it is composed of believers in Christ drawn from both categories (Exodus 33:16; 1 Chronicles 17:21, 22; 1 Corinthians 10:32; Ephesians 2:12). Thus, what first began as God's division of humanity into Jew and Gentile commenced after the cross into a division of Jew, Gentile, and church.

What Scriptures can we offer as proof of this? In Ephesians 2:11-12 Paul states, "Therefore remember that you who are *Gentiles* by birth . . . remember that at that time you were *separate from Christ* [before their conversion], excluded from citizenship in *Israel* and *foreigners to the covenants* of the promise, without hope and without God in the world." Here are three divisions of humanity: the Gentiles, the Jews, and the Christians made up of both converted Gentiles and converted Jews.

It is also clear from the Old Testament that Israel has a special relationship to God that is asserted to last forever. Exodus 33:16 states that the Jews are distinguished "from all the other people on the face of the earth." In 1 Chronicles 17:21-22 the writer asks,

> And who was like your people Israel—the one nation on earth whose God went out to redeem a people for Himself, and to make a name for yourself, and to perform great and awesome wonders by driving out nations from before your people, whom you redeemed from Egypt? You made your people Israel for your very own forever, and you, O Lord, have become their God.

Once again, what all this means is that there are now three divisions of mankind: Jews, Gentiles, and the church. Paul himself admonished that we were to not give offense either to "the Jews, nor to the Gentiles, nor to the church of God" (1 Corinthians 10:32).

This important distinction is consistently maintained throughout the Bible. These three groups exist side by side in the world today, and they will continue to do so until the end of the Millennium. Their importance to the interpretation of prophecy is noted by Dave Hunt: "We must keep a clear distinction between them and recognize that God deals with each group differently. This is fundamental when it comes to interpreting prophecy" (Hunt, *Global*, p. 27). Failure to make such a distinction will only bring confusion to prophetic interpretation.

132

In summary, prophecy becomes clouded in confusion if we fail to remember that the timing, manner, and purpose of the Lord's coming is different for "Jews, Gentiles, and the Church of God." The use of vague or ambiguous terms such as "Jesus is coming again" or the "the Return of Christ" or "Christ is coming" can cause misunderstanding. Coming for whom? Returning for whom? For the Church or for Israel and the nations? It makes a great difference. (Hunt, *Global*, p. 28)

For example, the rapture is not for unbelieving Jews or pagan Gentiles, but exclusively for believers composing the church. The Tribulation period is not for the church, but for unbelieving Israel and those in the Gentile world who will worship the Antichrist.

Finally, the second coming of Christ to earth is not primarily for believers in the church (who have already been raptured) but to take vengeance on those Gentiles who have turned against God and believed not the gospel and to rescue the nation of Israel from the Antichrist.

Thus, when prophecy is interpreted literally, an important division remains between Jew, Gentile, and church that helps us to see the logic of the pretribulation rapture. The rapture is for the church, to deliver it from God's wrath poured out on the earth during the Tribulation.

There is still another reason, perhaps the strongest, to accept a pretribulation rapture. This can be seen in messianic prophecy. Some who object to a pretribulation rapture have said that such a doctrine implies two comings of Christ or two phases of His second coming and that this is nowhere explicitly stated in Scripture.

But in fact, neither is the first and second coming of Christ clearly delineated in the Old Testament. Where in the Old Testament does it assert that Jesus will be born in a manger, and after his death, resurrection, and ascension to heaven, many years later return to earth as a triumphant king? Nowhere. But even though no prophet explicitly stated this, the implication was evident. Why? Because it was impossible to put into one event what the Hebrew prophets had said concerning the coming of the Messiah. For example, the prophets in one place predicted that the Messiah would be killed (Isaiah 53:8) and yet He would establish a millennial kingdom and rule it forever (Isaiah 11:4-12; 24:3, 23; 60:11-22; 65:18-25). In another place the prophets say He would be rejected by Israel, yet He would be accepted by them and forever reign on David's throne.

Isaiah predicted the Messiah would be cut off from the land of the living, buried in a rich man's grave, and yet also live. However, can anyone harmonize these ideas? Such dichotomies require that there be two comings—Jesus' first coming, where He dies on the cross and pays for our sins, and Jesus' second coming, still in the future, where He will return to rule as the mighty king. There is simply no other way to reconcile what are otherwise contradictory prophecies.

But, if the Old Testament prophecies concerning the Messiah's coming to earth require us to hold by two appearances, we find that the same is true for the prophecies concerning Christ's second coming. The verses suggest two parts to that which is spoken of as the return of Christ to earth. Christ must first come to rapture the church and then come to deliver the world from total destruction. "Just as it was impossible to put together into one event what the Old Testament said about the Messiah's coming, so it is equally impossible to put together into one event what the New Testament says about His coming again" (Hunt, *Global*, p. 216). For example:

> Christ's Coming to earth to "stand in that day upon the Mount of Olives" (Zechariah 14:4) is hardly compatible with the promise we will "meet the Lord in the air: and so shall we ever be with the Lord" (1 Thessalonians 4:17). His Coming "with ten thousands of His saints to execute judgment upon all [the ungodly]" (Jude 1:14, 15) could hardly be the same happening as "the dead shall be raised incorruptible, and we shall be changed" (1 Corinthians 15:52). His visible Coming in power and great glory like lightning streaking across the sky (Matthew 24:27) when "every eye shall see Him" (Revelation 1:7) hardly seems to be describing the same thing as "I will come again and receive you unto myself, that where I am, there ye may be also" (John 14:3). . . . Not only are the two tasks that Christ returns to accomplish so diverse that they do not fit well into one event, but the conditions prevailing upon earth when He returns clearly describe *two different time periods*. Christ stated, for example, that His Coming

would be during a time of peace, prosperity, business and pleasure—a time when the last thing the world expects is judgment [Matthew 24:37-39. In these verses] . . . Jesus could hardly be describing His Second Coming at the end of the Great Tribulation after God's wrath has brought destruction and the world's armies are in the midst of the battle of Armageddon. . . . Clearly there yet *must be two Comings*. Nor have we exhausted the reasons for this view by any means. (Hunt, *Global*, pp. 214-15)

In light of this evidence, it is impossible to reconcile all the events describing the second coming of Christ as occurring at the same moment.

In summary, then, our arguments for a pretribulational rapture are as follows: (1) the thousand-year millennial reign of Christ is required from a reading of Revelation 20:2-5; (2) the Tribulation preceding the return of Christ to earth is required by a reading of 2 Thessalonians 2:3-8; (3) the different descriptions of Christ's return require a distinction between the rapture (1 Thessalonians 4:16-18) and Christ's return to earth after the Tribulation (2 Thessalonians 2:3-8); and (4) the doctrine of imminency demands that all Christians be ready now for Christ to return (Matthew 28:42-44).

Do the Ancient Prophecies Fit the Modern Facts?

Could the rapture happen right now? Yes, it could. (See also the discussion in chapter 14.) It is the events unraveling during our generation that signify the possibility that the return of Christ may be near. If it can be shown that these events parallel the events Christ taught would signal that His return to earth was near, then this logically would require us to hold that the rapture is even nearer.

In Matthew 24 Jesus predicted that certain signs would precede his return—false Christs, wars and rumors of wars, nation rising against nation, and famines and earthquakes in various places (Matthew 24:4-7). But He identified them as "the beginning of birth pains" (v. 8). Persecution will also occur against believers and the gospel will be preached throughout the world. There will be "great distress, unequalled from the beginning of the world until now—and never to be equalled again" (Matthew 24:21).

After giving His disciples these signs that would signal the nearness of His coming (v. 3), Jesus said, "Now learn this lesson from the fig tree: As soon as its twigs get tender and its leaves come out, you know that summer is near. Even so, *when you see all these things, you know that it [His return] is near*, right at the door" (Matthew 24:32-33).

If the very things that Christ warned us about are happening, then His coming is near. Concerning these signs, Dave Hunt writes: "Certain signs . . . [indicating] the nearness of the Second Coming may cast their shadows far enough in advance to tell the church that the Rapture must be soon" (Hunt, *Global*, p. 42). According to Hunt,

> It is exciting to note that no generation has ever had solid biblical reason for believing that it was living in the last of the last days preceding the Second Coming of Christ—no generation until ours. . . . For the first time in history, all of the signs heralding the Second Coming could occur at any moment. In fact, the present generation—unlike any generation before it—has more than sufficient reason for believing that the Second Coming is very near. (Hunt, *Global*, pp. 42-43)

How many of the signs of the second coming are casting their shadows before them now? Could our generation be the first ever that has seen any of these shadows? We believe the answer is yes.

First, there is today the possibility of the destruction of all life on earth. As we just saw, this was predicted by Jesus in Matthew 24:22 as a frightening reality for the days immediately preceding His return. We all know that we have the nuclear capability to destroy every living person on the globe—several times over. Jesus' statement has been a mystery to everyone living prior to our generation. But it is no mystery to us. Unfortunately it is all too clear.

Second, our generation is the first to understand how the Bible could predict that no one on earth would be able to engage in economic transactions without the special identifying mark termed "the mark of the beast." In the book of Revelation, the apostle John prophesied that a world ruler would control the entire earth—not just militarily and politically—but economically as well:

> He also forced everyone, small and great, rich and poor, free and slave, to receive a mark on his right hand or on his forehead, so that no one could buy or sell unless he had the mark, which is the name of the beast [Antichrist] or the number of his name. . . . His number is 666. (Revelation 13:16, 18)

If no one on earth is able to buy or sell anything without the mark of the beast, then this demands the possibility of a centralized, interdependent financial apparatus. Never in the entire history of mankind has this happened—until now. Today we have communication satellites, worldwide electronic banking networks, and vastly sophisticated computers regulating the stock market and international transactions. In *Encounters with the Future: A Forecast of Life into the 21st Century*, Marvin Cetron, president of Forecasting International and a graduate professor at MIT, predicts, "We will soon enter a checkless and cashless society" (p. 27).

In fact, it is probably just a matter of time until the world will follow the example of the twelve European nations that have agreed to use one monetary system. Here we see one more prophecy concerning the end times that no generation prior to ours could understand, much less imagine as being applicable in its own day (Hunt, *Global*, p. 43). One social commentator informs us more about this:

> Right now, as you are reading this letter, a U.S. company is perfecting a silicon computer chip that can be implanted under the skin. And this chip can be read by scanners identical to the ones in your supermarket.

In fact, company documents obtained by [us] state that the chip has been "developed in cooperation with government agencies" to solve the age-old problem of "providing positive identification of equipment, animals and people."

And by combining this new technology with that of electronic banking . . . which planners boast will "lead to the destruction of cash and the birth of the cashless society . . . you can quickly realize how close the Mark of the Beast may be!

In fact, Terry Galanoy—the former Director of Communications for VISA International—has issued this warning:

Protesting too loudly about it isn't going to help either, because the disturbance you kick up is going to end up in one of your files. And on that come-and-get-it day, when we're all totally and completely dependent on our card—OR WHATEVER SURVIVAL DEVICE MIGHT REPLACE IT—you might be left all alone without one. Now, doesn't that remind you of Revelation 13:16-17? (*The Omega Letter*)

Third, our world is also the first in human history that is capable of being woven into a united world religion. Put simply, it is human nature to worship something—be it God, a philosophy, or self. Today, literally millions of people turn out in mass rallies to honor highly charismatic leaders such as the Pope or Communist rulers. Undoubtedly, there will be future charismatic leaders who will be placed on a pedestal or even worshiped.

Thus, it is not impossible that at a future date, the Antichrist, the most charismatic political leader the world will ever see, could influence and manipulate the hearts and minds of men to worship him. Because of his incredible miracles and military power the Bible tells us that "the whole world was astonished and followed the Beast [Antichrist] . . . and they also *worshiped* the beast and asked, 'Who is like the beast? Who can make war against him?'" (Revelation 13:4).

If a seemingly benevolent, yet powerful and dramatic, miracle-working individual became the military, political, and economic head of the world, there is little reason to think he could not become its spiritual head as well.

But the Antichrist will also have a powerful accomplice, a False Prophet, who will himself perform astounding miracles and confirm the authority of the Antichrist: "And he performed great and miraculous signs, even causing fire to come down from heaven to earth in full view of men. Because of the signs he was given power to do on behalf of the first beast [Antichrist], he deceived the inhabitants of the earth" (Revelation 13:13-14). Thus, just as it is now possible for the world to be economically and politically united, for the first time in human history it is also possible that it could be *spiritually* united (see chapter 14).

But there is more. In all of human history we have never before had the ability to communicate the gospel to the entire world just as Jesus predicted would occur shortly before the end: "And this gospel of the kingdom will be preached in the whole world as a testimony to all nations, and then the end will come" (Matthew 24:14).

During the 1991 Gulf War, the entire world was able to tune in to CNN via satellite to watch the events unfolding. The gospel also is being proclaimed around the world using the latest technology. For example, in December 1990, Billy Graham spoke to 100 million people via satellite hookup from the Orient. Given the combined impact of all satellite ministries and other evangelism we are close to fulfilling the prediction of Jesus.

Finally, Jesus' solemn predictions (Matthew 24:5, 11, 24) about false prophets doing false miracles have found fulfillment in our generation unlike that of any other. The apostle Paul stated in 1 Timothy 4:1 that "the Spirit clearly says that in later times some will abandon the faith and follow deceiving spirits and things taught by demons."

In all its myriad forms, the occult is now a multi-billion dollar worldwide business. If we consider that there are almost one billion believers in astrology, several hundred million believers in various forms of spiritism, and several hundred million believers in other forms of the occult, then no one can deny that today demonism is dramatically influencing the world (Ankerberg, Weldon, *Guides*; *Occult*, pp. 9-10; *Astrology*, p. 8).

Today, there are literally tens of millions of book copies in circulation dictated by numerous spirits through their human mediums. We documented (Ankerberg, Weldon, *New Age*; *Doctor*; *Guides*; *Occult*; *Astrology*) this powerful influence of modern occultism in the U.S. in another publication:

In America there are thousands of channelers. Millions of followers seek out the channelers for advice or read the literature given by the spirits through their channelers. Based on the sales of channeled literature, tapes, and seminars, channeling in America is a hundred-million dollar a year enterprise. Some have referred to America's growing interest in channeling as having "epidemic" proportions. . . . The endorsement of channeling by famous television and movie stars is making the practice socially acceptable. Examples of stars who have this kind of influence are Shirley MacLaine, Linda Evans (of "Dynasty"), Michael York (of "Romeo and Juliet") and others.

Actress Sharon Gless, who plays "Cagney" on the hit TV series "Cagney and Lacey," won a 1987 "Emmy" for her role on the series. In her acceptance speech, she told tens of millions that her success was due to "Lazaris," a spirit entity who speaks through medium Jach Pursel.

Another area showing the popularity of channeling is its growing influence in the sciences and other disciplines. The spirits are speaking out of their human hosts, giving information that is applied to theories in psychology, to the practice of medicine, to the investigation of parapsychology, to the study of physics, to the application of sociology, and to the development of new ideas in theology, archaeology, and other disciplines. (Ankerberg, Weldon, *Guides*, pp. 7-8)

It has only been in our generation that television can be beamed to millions of people showing channelers and their spirit guides.

If the trend continues, the spirits could, through human mediums, offer actual classes on television and video tapes. The more powerful "channelers" would have live trance interviews or be "taped-in-trance" and the material played back on educational television or through other media. To millions of Americans the spirits are already accepted as "wise," instructive and as entertaining as human teachers. If hundreds of millions of dollars are now being spent to listen to spirits on cassette and video, this means the age of electronic spirit contact is already here.

Even the spirits themselves are actively promoting the idea of "educational" spiritism. Consider the following statement by the spirit being called "Mentor" who speaks through Meredith Lady Young. The spirit has reached thousands through mediumistic seminars conducted before large audiences. Ms. Young stated that "Mentor" told her "it will not be long before 'channeling' will be considered the norm rather than the exception. . . . humankind will enter the New Age of awareness, learning to integrate the mystical and the practical. One's 'teachers' or 'spirit guides' will be as common as one's professors at a university. The professor will teach mathematics and the spiritual 'teacher' will enlighten." (Ankerberg, Weldon, *New Age*, p. 17)

Kevin Ryerson is one of the more articulate channelers and has appeared on dozens of radio and TV shows. On these shows he offers live interviews with his spirit guides. Another channeler is J. Z. Knight who channels "Ramtha." . . . Knight has sold almost a thousand hours of "Ramtha's" video and audio tapes. Like many channelers, she is now a multi-millionaire. Another channeler is Jach Pursel who channels "Lazaris." He runs a multi-million dollar corporation entitled "Concept-Synergy." This corporation is dedicated to making Lazaris' teachings available to thousands of other people. (Ankerberg, Weldon, *Guides*, p. 10)

Thousands of new cults and occultic practices have tentacles that are ensnaring literally hundreds of millions around the globe. Some have argued that our modern era is the first in history to experience the nature and extent of cultism and occultism to this advanced degree. If the shadows of events foretelling Christ's return are now beginning to appear, then those same shadows signify that the rapture of the church must be even nearer.

18

The Emergence of a New World Leader Who Will Be the Ultimate Personal Communicator— The Antichrist

[We require] a man of sufficient stature to hold the allegiance of all people. . . . Send us such a man and be he God or devil we will receive him.

Henri Spaack
Early planner of the Common Market

What Do the Ancient Prophecies Predict?

Daniel 7:23-25 (530 B.C.):

He [the angel] gave me this explanation: "The fourth beast is a fourth kingdom that will appear on earth. It will be different from all the other kingdoms and will devour the whole earth, trampling it down and crushing it. The ten horns are ten kings who will come from this kingdom. After them another king will rise, different from the earlier ones; he will subdue three kings. He will speak against the Most High and oppress his saints.

Revelation 13:5-9 (A.D. 70-90):

> The beast was given a mouth to utter proud words and blasphe-
> mies and to exercise his authority for forty-two months. He
> opened his mouth to blaspheme God, and to slander his name and
> his dwelling place [the restored Temple] and those who live in
> heaven. He was given power to make war against the saints and
> to conquer them. And he was given authority over every tribe,
> people, language and nation. All inhabitants of the earth will
> worship the beast—all whose names have not been written in the
> book of life belonging to the Lamb that was slain from the
> creation of the world. He who has an ear, let him hear.

Revelation 17:12-13 (A.D. 70-90):

> The ten horns you saw are ten kings who have not yet received a
> kingdom, but who for one hour will receive authority as kings
> along with the beast. They have one purpose and will give their
> power and authority to the beast.

The above prophecies refer to a world empire of the last
days that will rule the entire earth. Through symbolism and
imagery the ancient prophets predicted that the world would
finally end up living under a world dictator. Both the world
empire and its leader are described as beasts.

The prophet Daniel, writing about 530 B.C., described four
world kingdoms, the last of which is also future and will rule the
entire earth. In Daniel 7, ten kings or powers will emerge out of
the predicted fourth world empire, which is symbolically described as the fourth beast. But this power is unlike any other:
"It was different from all the former beasts, and it had ten
horns" (Daniel 7:7).

In Revelation 17:13, we are told that ten powers or nations
will give their authority to "the Beast," who is described else-
where as the Antichrist, the one who opposes God, persecutes his
people, and finally displays himself in the restored Jewish
Temple, demanding that he be worshiped as God (2 Thessalonians 2:4). The book of Revelation tells us, "And he was given

authority over every tribe, people, language and nation. All the inhabitants of the earth will worship the beast" (Revelation 13:7).

In addition, the Antichrist performs "great and miraculous signs." He deceives "the inhabitants of the earth," he forces all who will not worship him "to be killed," and "he also force[s] everyone, small and great, rich and poor, free and slave, to receive a mark on his right hand or on his forehead, so that no one could buy or sell unless he had the mark, which is the name of the beast or the number of his name" (Revelation 13:16-17). Many people today think that several economic, political and military conditions are moving the world in the direction of a one-world government. Whether the U.N. will play a role in this future world government remains unclear, but none can deny that a United Europe will shortly become a major world power. This fact will assist the process of making the world even more economically interdependent.

Regardless of the form of the coming one-world government, many think it is now on the way and that current world conditions are leading in that direction. Below we see the possibility for the predicted scenario of events to transpire.

Do the Ancient Prophecies Fit the Modern Facts?

A Revived and Powerful Europe

No one on earth could have predicted the events that began the 1990s. In fact, no one would even have tried. But the unprecedented German reunification and liberation of Soviet satellites in Eastern Europe completely startled everyone. Europe is now in a position to become a militarily powerful and increasingly economically dominant force. A United States of Europe would become the most powerful political, military, and economic force in the world.

But without energy from the Middle East, Europe would grind to a halt. One reason the French and British fought against

Iraq was to preserve their Middle East oil supplies. European unity helps move the world toward increasing interdependence. Further, its heavy reliance on Arab oil and susceptibility to Middle East sensitivities guarantees that a United Europe would consider its interest in the Middle East vital. Even today, many European governments are calling for some kind of resolution to the problems of that area.

An Emerging "New World Order" and the Increasing Need for a "Benevolent" World Ruler or Dictator

The Antichrist could be alive today. Increasing pressures on several fronts are moving toward a one-world dictatorship. Fifty years ago this was unthinkable. But anyone who says this could never happen today would be foolish.

For example, Robert Payne is an authority on dictators, having written definitive volumes on Hitler, Mao Tse-T'ung, Ho Chi Minh and others. As far back as 1973 in an interview with Dick Spangler on KGIL radio in San Fernando, California, Payne stated his belief that "all over the world"—in Africa, Asia, large sections of Europe and the U.S.—there was the possibility of "one man taking over the whole thing and ruling simply by command."

In his *Warning to the West* Alexander Solzhenitsyn observes, "We are approaching a major turning point in world history, in the history of civilization. It has already been noted by specialists in various areas" (Solzhenitsyn, p. 79). One of those specialists is Alvin Tofler, author of *Future Shock* and other books. He observes in his *The Eco-Spasm Report* that "the nation-state can no longer cope with the basic problems posed by the shift towards super-industrialism" and that "what is happening, no more, no less, is the breakdown of industrial civilization on the planet and the first fragmentary appearance of a wholly new and dramatic different social order: a super-industrial civilization that will be technological, but no longer industrial" (pp. 74, 3).

President Bush and other world leaders are currently engaging in a movement toward what they call a "new world order."

In many quarters we find the willingness to consider the advantages of a world leader. For example, the most influential person associated with the third largest political party in Japan, Daisaku Ikeda, summarized eminent historian Arnold Toynbee's recent views and offered his own comments:

> A dictator with outstanding leadership ability may be a necessity in the course of world unification. You expect to see the rise of a new world religion that will serve as a catalyst for the spiritual unity of all nations. . . . I feel that a precedent for future world unity may be found in the current European attempt to achieve an intracontinental federation of nations. (Toynbee, Ikeda, p. 243)

According to Edgar James, one of the early planners of the Common Market, Henri Spaak, observed that many Europeans are looking for "a man of sufficient stature to hold the allegiance of all people and to lift us out of the economic morass into which we are sinking. Send us such a man and be he god or devil, we will receive him" (James, "Prophecy," p. 44).

In *The 2025 Report*, Cambridge educated Norman Macrae, deputy editor of *The Economist*, noted, "It is clear that we are approaching a period when there must be a sea [massive, fundamental] change in the whole concept of nationality" (p. 246).

In *The Third Wave*, seminal author Alvin Toffler observes:

> The Third Wave [i.e., tidal wave of change in history] gives rise to groups with larger than national interests. These form the base of the emerging globalist ideology sometimes called "planetary consciousness."
>
> This consciousness is shared by multinational executives, long-haired environmental campaigners, financiers, revolutionaries, intellectuals, poets, and painters, not to mention members of the Trilateral Commission. I have even had a famous U.S. four-star general assure me that "the nation-state is dead." Globalism presents itself as more than an ideology serving the interests of a limited group. Precisely as nationalism claimed to speak for the whole nation, globalism claims to speak for the whole world. And its appearance is seen as an evolutionary necessity—a step closer

to a "cosmic consciousness" that would embrace the heavens as well.

In sum, therefore, at every level, from economics and politics to organization and ideology, we are witnessing a devastating attack, from within and without, on that pillar of Second Wave civilization: the nation-state. (p. 342)

In his *July 20, 2019: Life in the 21st Century*, celebrated writer Arthur C. Clarke closes with the following words:

The long-heralded Global Village is almost upon us, but it will last for only a flickering moment in the history of mankind. Before we even realize that it has come, it will be superseded—by the Global Family.

And when we have the Global Family ["the United States of Earth"], we will no longer need the United Nations.

But until then . . . (p. 276)

All this demonstrates that the world is increasingly prepared to accept a future leader. Recall that in our last chapter we discussed the biblical predictions of a rapture. This rapture could play an important role in the political emergence of the Antichrist. Hardly anyone can fathom the results of the instantaneous disappearance of hundreds of millions of people around the world. Here a feasible connection could exist between the event of the rapture and the rise to power of the Antichrist.

Ideas alone have only rarely changed the world. It is ideas presented by incredibly dynamic and compelling personal communicators that really change the world—leaders such as Marx, Hitler, Mussolini, Stalin, Martin Luther King, and Ronald Reagan. What will unite the world will not be a mere idea but the combination of the right man with the right idea:

These forms of unity—commercial, political, military, and religious—cannot, however, be expected to happen by accident. In all of history, unity has been based on two major considerations: a principle which is compelling but somewhat abstract, and a leader who is concrete and charismatic. People rarely gather or exercise great passions over mere principle or a point of doctrine. However, when that IDEOLOGY or spiritual point of view is embodied in a great personal communicator, then . . . PRESTO, a catalytic conversion takes place. (Breese, pp. 29-30)

Could we have a leader like that today? After the Gulf War, all the TV networks were reporting that George Bush's popularity rating was more than 85 percent—higher than that of any president in American history. Why was Bush so popular? It was because of world events, a stunning military victory. He pulled the nations together for a common goal—to bring peace to the Middle East. If Bush did this through a major military victory, imagine the popularity of the man who would first solidify the nations of Europe into a great economic power and then accomplished much more. What if he actually brought—or seemed to bring—a lasting peace to the Middle East? What do you think his popularity rating would be worldwide? When President Bush united twenty-six nations, worked brilliantly through the United Nations, even got Russia on his side, and then got the job done, we saw a demonstration of the popularity a future worldwide leader will command if he uses his skills and abilities to lead the world where it has never been—politically, militarily, and economically united. Further, if one adds the supernatural factor, the biblical predictions are no longer so fantastic. They are credible.

If the Bible says that similar although greater events really are to happen when the Antichrist appears on the scene, it is not surprising that all the world will give its allegiance to this man.

But the Bible goes on to say the whole world will not just give its allegiance but will worship this imposing figure. But because it does so it will pay terrible price because it will really be worshiping Satan, who is the real power behind him (2 Thessalonians 2:9). God warns that anyone who worships the Antichrist will suffer the consequences:

If anyone worships the beast and his image and receives his mark on the forehead or on the hand, he, too, will drink of the wine of God's fury, which has been poured full strength into the cup of his wrath. He will be tormented with burning sulfur in the presence of the holy angels and of the Lamb. And the smoke of their torment rises forever and ever. There is no rest day or night for those who worship the beast and his image, or for anyone who receives the mark of his name. (Revelation 14:9-11)

The Bible envisions a world political leader of unparalleled communication, cunning, power, and evil. But Christians will not have to experience directly what this man does to the world. That is one reason the doctrine of the rapture is a blessed hope for the Christian.

In conclusion, the current events would seem to bear out the Bible's prediction of a major end-time world power headed by a single leader who unites the entire earth in some form of political, economic, and religious system. As we will now see, Israel is destined to remain a key player in world history. The Bible predicts that at some point in the future, a coalition of nations will attack Israel. Further, the Bible also predicts that the last great war of the world, called Armageddon, will be fought in the Middle East. It is to those prophecies that we now turn.

19
The Coming Russian Invasion of the Middle East

Scatter the nations who delight in war.

Psalm 68:30

What Are the Ancient Prophecies?

Ezekiel 38:8-9 (580 B.C.):

After many days you [the Northern Power] will be called to arms. In future years, you will invade a land that has recovered from war, whose people were gathered from many nations to the mountains of Israel, which had long been desolate. They had been brought out from the nations, and now all of them live in safety. You and all your troops and the many nations with you will go up, advancing like a storm; you will be like a cloud covering the land.

Ezekiel 38:15-16 (580 B.C.):

> You will come from your place in the far north, you and many
> nations with you, all of them riding on horses, a great horde, a
> mighty army. You will advance against my people Israel like a
> cloud that covers the land. In days to come, O Gog, I will bring
> you against my land, so that nations may know me when I show
> myself holy through you before their eyes.

Ezekiel 38:18-23 (580 B.C.):

> This is what will happen in that day: When Gog attacks the land
> of Israel, my hot anger will be aroused, declares the Sovereign
> Lord. In my zeal and fiery wrath, I declare that at that time there
> shall be a great earthquake in the land of Israel. The fish of the
> sea, the birds of the air, the beasts of the field, every creature that
> moves along the ground, and all the people on the face of the
> earth will tremble at my presence. The mountains will be over-
> turned, the cliffs will crumble and every wall will fall to the
> ground. I will summon a sword against Gog on all my mountains,
> declares the Sovereign Lord. Every man's sword will be against
> his brother. I will execute judgment upon him with plague and
> bloodshed; I will pour down torrents of rain, hailstones and
> burning sulfur on him and on his troops and on the many nations
> with him. And so I will show my greatness and my holiness, and
> I will make myself known in the sight of many nations. Then they
> will know that I am the Lord.

Ezekiel 38-39 describes an attack of Israel by a northern
power. Whether the power described is Russia or not, this
prophecy clearly indicates a great enemy "from the far north"
(38:6; 39:2). An army composed of itself and "many nations"
(38:6, 9, 15) will brutally attack and overwhelm Israel (38:14-16).

But God Himself will execute judgment upon those nations
and destroy them on the mountains of Israel (38:18–39:6). There
will be so many bodies that months will be required to bury
them, and the burial procedures will be so vast as to inhibit
travelers (39:11-12). Weapons will be so numerous they will be

used as fuel for years (39:9-10). "Then the nations will know that I the Lord am the Holy One in Israel. It is coming! It will surely take place, declares the Sovereign Lord. This is the day I have spoken of" (39:7-8).

But how do we know this prophecy is still future? We know because it has not yet been literally fulfilled. The fact that many events are described that have never occurred in Israel prove that this prophecy, if it is to be interpreted literally, must be future. For example, in Ezekiel 38:18-23 God describes the destruction of those invading armies by supernatural means, and that has never happened in history.

Can we determine if this northern power really is Russia? The simple fact is that there is only one nation to the far north of Israel—Russia. One only need check a map. Russia is the only possible major enemy to Israel's far north having the ability to mount the kind of campaign and results described. Further, there are good linguistic reasons for accepting the identification of Russia as this northern power. Some of those are described in Thomas McCall's and Zola Levitt's *The Coming Russian Invasion of Israel* and other sources (Lindsey, *Earth*; Walvoord, *Armageddon*; *Prophecy*; Levitt, *Satan*). Biblical scholar Arnold Fruchtenbaum agrees with their assessment:

> [In Ezekiel 38:1-4] attention is centered on *Gog*, leader of the *land of Magog*. He is the prince of *Rosh, Meshech* and *Tubal*. Who Gog will be can only be determined at the time of the invasion for "Gog" is not a proper name but a title for the ruler of Magog just as the terms Pharaoh, Kaiser, and Czar were titles for rulers and not proper names. Whoever is ruling this alliance at the time of the invasion will be Ezekiel's Gog. The identification of Magog, Rosh, Meschech and Tubal is to be determined from the fact that these tribes of the ancient world occupied the areas of modern day Russia. Magog, Meschech and Tubal were between the Black and Caspian Seas which today is southern Russia. The tribes of Meschech and Tubal later gave names to cities that today bear the names of Moscow, the capital, and Tobolsk, the major city in the Urals in Siberia. Rosh was in what is now northern Russia. The name Rosh is the basis for the modern name Russia.

These names, then, cover the modern territories of northern and southern Russia in Europe and Siberia to the east in Asia. The modern nation of the Soviet Union encompasses all these areas of Ezekiel.

As if to avoid any further possible doubt, verse six adds that these come from *the uttermost parts of the north*. This is repeated in 38:15 and 39:2. From Israel the uttermost parts of the north is Russia with Moscow being almost a straight line due north from Jerusalem. (Fruchtenbaum, p. 70)

The following discussion by three leading interpreters of prophecy, John Walvoord, Dwight Pentecost, and Charles Ryrie offers additional relevant material:

[Walvoord] But the fact that today, for the first time in history, Russia is such a major power and Israel is back in the land makes it possible for the first time since the early years of the Christian period for such a prophecy to have a reasonable fulfillment. Prior to this, Israel wasn't in the land and Russia wasn't a great nation. Both of these factors had to be there in order for the prophecies to be fulfilled.

[Pentecost] Daniel 11:40 mentions an invasion of the land of Israel by the King of the North and the King of the South. Now the King of the South all through Daniel 11 is a reference to Egypt. This strongly suggests that at the end time Egypt, and perhaps the other Arab nations, will be allied with or under the authority of Russia. That gives significance to the spread of Russian influence in the Middle East today.

[Ryrie] The identification of Magog, to which Dr. Walvoord referred in Ezekiel 38, has since the time of Josephus been placed in the area north and east of the Black Sea and the Aral Sea. The Black Sea is north of Turkey, but the Aral Sea is totally surrounded by Russian territory, so I think there is no question as to the location of this hoard [sic] of people that will descend on Israel. (Walvoord, *Prophecy*, p. 5)

The northern powers' confederates in the attack against Israel are listed in Ezekiel 38:5-6, given by their ancient names and/or geographical regions. They include Persia, Cush, Put,

Gomer and Beth Togarmah. According to Fruchtenbaum, and many other scholars, these nations are the modern Iran, Ethiopia, Somalia, Germany, and Armenia (part of Russia), respectively:

> But Russia is not alone in the invasion of Israel. . . . Involved in the confederacy is Persia or present day Iran. . . .
>
> Another nation involved is called Cush. There were two places that had that name. One was in Mesopotamia (Genesis 2:13). But all other usages of this word refer to Ethiopia. While looking at current events, it is tempting to identify it with the Mesopotamian countries of Syria and Iraq, consistency with the usage of the word Cush elsewhere in the Scriptures demands its identification with Ethiopia. Current events must never be the means of interpreting the Scriptures, but the Scriptures must interpret current events. . . .
>
> Put is mentioned next which is not Libya for which the name Lub would be used, but Somaliland or Somalia. Somalia borders Ethiopia.
>
> This is followed by Gomer located in present-day Germany. . . . The last name is Togarmah which is present-day Armenia and is totally within Russia. (Fruchtenbaum, p. 70-71)*

From all of this it is clear that the Bible is calling for an invasion of Israel from the north. The Bible points out that the northern power will include not only Russia but other countries as well, such as modern day Iran, Ethiopia, Somalia and, incredibly, Germany.

Do the Ancient Prophecies Fit the Modern Facts?

For this information, see chapters 4 and 10.

---

*For a discussion of why the use of ancient names of some now extinct nations does not undermine a literal interpretation but merely refers to their modern counterparts, see Tan, pp. 224-26.

20

What Events Happen During the Tribulation Period and Lead to the Final World War— The Battle of Armageddon?

The most prevalent opinion among our so confused contemporaries seems to be that tomorrow will be wonderful—that is, unless it is indescribably terrible, or unless indeed there just isn't any.

Joseph Wood Krutch

We are rapidly entering the most fearful period in human history.

Hal Lindsey
Road, p. 282

What Are the Ancient Prophecies?

Revelation 16:12-16 (A.D. 70-90):

> The sixth angel poured out his bowl on the great river Euphrates, and its water was dried up to prepare the way for the kings from the East. Then I saw . . . [the] spirits of demons performing miraculous signs, and they go out to the kings of the whole world,

to gather them for the battle on the great day of God Almighty. . . . They gathered the kings together to the place that in Hebrew is called Armageddon.

Zechariah 14:2-3; 12:9; 14:12-14 (500 B.C.)

I will gather all the nations to Jerusalem to fight against it; the city will be captured, . . . then the Lord will go out and fight against those nations, as he fights in the day of battle. . . . On that day, I will set out to destroy all the nations that attack Jerusalem. . . . This is the plague with which the Lord will strike all the nations that fought against Jerusalem: Their flesh will rot while they are still standing on their feet, their eyes will rot in their sockets, and their tongues will rot in their mouths. On that day men will be strickened by the Lord with great panic.

According to prophecy, Israel will be surrounded by enemies on all sides:

The Scriptures picture armies from the north, the south, and the east fighting it out in the Holy Land up to the very time of the second coming of Christ. Zechariah 14 describes house to house fighting in Jerusalem at the very time of Christ's return. (Walvoord, *Prophecy*, p. 5)

The great countries of the world are all [described as] fighting it out for power and Israel is caught in the middle of the conflict. This is the great war that Christ is going to stop and interrupt by His second coming. Revelation 19 makes it clear He will put to death all of the opposing armies because they are all against Him. (Walvoord, *Prophecy*, p. 6)

Jesus described the Great Tribulation in Matthew 24. "For then there will be great distress, unequaled from the beginning of the world until now—and never to be equaled again. If those days had not been cut short, no one would survive, but for the sake of the elect, those days will be shortened" (Matthew 24:21-22).

It is the second coming of Christ Himself that will cut those days short and prevent complete world annihilation. The incredible destruction wrought upon the world, which chooses to worship Satan rather than God, is revealed in Revelation 6-19. Consider some of the horrible events that these chapters indicate will happen during the Tribulation:

- initially one-third of the earth and its oceans and rivers are destroyed (8:7-11)

- demonic creatures torment men for five months (9:1-11)

- war and plagues kill one-third of mankind (9:15-10; 11:6, 10)

- ugly, painful sores are placed on everyone who worships the Antichrist (16:2-10)

- the remaining two-thirds of the sea dies (16:3)

- the sun scorches people on the earth who are "seared with intense heat" (16:9)

- one-hundred pound hailstones fall on the earth in a "terrible plague" (16:21)

These are only some of the judgments of this particular time in human history—a time that will never be paralleled.

The Tribulation period is composed of seven years, the first three and one-half years constitute a period of apparent relative peace when the Antichrist signs a peace treaty with Israel. The last three and one-half years involve massive destruction that is described as the Great Tribulation. This leads to the final world conflict of Armageddon.

Armageddon, of course, is a term used throughout the centuries to depict the horrors of war. It is based on the description given in the book of Revelation. The name Armageddon comes from Har (Mount) and Mageddon (Megiddo). Throughout history the area in which Armageddon is to be fought has frequently been a place of slaughter. Even Napoleon is reported to have stood upon the hill of Megiddo. He recalled the book of Revelation as he looked over the expansive valley and stated,

"All the armies of the world could maneuver for battle here" (Lindsey, *Earth*, p. 164).

In essence, the Great Tribulation, which leads to Armageddon, will be a time of unparalleled judgment upon the world for its evil. The world will experience the full wrath of God (Revelation 14:19). Revelation 14:20 describes a river of blood four and one-half to five feet deep—even to the horses' bridles.

This river of blood will cover 200 miles, the entire length of Palestine today. In other words, the entire land will be covered with war from the valley of Megiddo in the north to the land of Edom in the south. "This entire area will be covered with the blood of nations" (James, *Arabs*, p. 86).

There will be four major groups, or confederacies, of nations that will surround Israel during the Great Tribulation. It is highly significant that the present world scene parallels these predicted end-time powers. One great power block will be located to the west of Israel in the general area of the ancient Roman Empire.

Apparently, the Antichrist will begin by subjugating three nations (Daniel 7:8) with seven others granting Him their allegiance: "The ten horns you saw are ten kings who have not yet received a kingdom, but who for one hour will receive authority as kings along with the beast [Antichrist]. They have one purpose and will give their power and authority to the beast" (Revelation 17:12-13). Once the Antichrist is head of this ten-nation, or power, confederacy, he will make a treaty with Israel guaranteeing its protection. But he will later break it and enter Israel for his own purposes. He will persecute the people of God, enter the restored Temple and demand to be worshiped as God.

Another power block will come from the "far North." We have already described this power and the possibility that it could be Russia.

The third power block is said to come from the east of Israel and is described as "the kings from the East." This power block is described in Revelation as the sixth bowl of judgment. Because the term is plural ("kings"), it is likely this is a confederacy of nations. According to Revelation 9:13-16, the size of this nation's army is an astonishing 200 million men. Thus, the kings of the East probably refer to the masses of Asia. Consider Japan, India, China and the complex of nations known today as the Pacific Rim. Japan and other nations are actively seeking to unite this Asian confederacy into a world power.

Nevertheless, this massive army is said to be demonically instituted and is gathered "together to the place that in Hebrew is called Armageddon" (Revelation 16:12, 14, 16). Significantly, the Bible teaches that the Euphrates River, so prominent in the 1991 Gulf War, will actually be dried up to prepare the way for these kings from the east (Revelation 16:12).

The fourth power block concerns a southern confederacy referred to in Daniel 11. The Arab nations may fit here, in that many of them are south of Israel. The king of the south (Daniel 11:5) is Egypt. Egypt plays an important role, at least indirectly. But it will eventually be defeated (Ezekiel 30:3-4, 13; Daniel 11:42).

Nevertheless, the early stages for this final war will apparently be initiated when Egypt will push against Israel, encouraging the northern confederacy to attack as well (Daniel 11:40):

> After Egypt pushes at Israel and Russia and her allies come against Israel, God will destroy the northern armies in the mountains of Palestine. Until then, there will be a balance of world power, but a miracle [of judgment] will break that balance. Perhaps this is why the western confederacy, the revived Roman Empire, will then move into the "Beautiful Land" (Daniel 11:41).
>
> This group of nations, lead by the Antichrist, will take the treasures of the land, even "all the riches of Egypt" (Daniel 11:43). There is speculation that there may be oil in the western part of Egypt to which this may refer. In any event, this is also the time when the Antichrist will put himself in the Temple and call himself God. (2 Thessalonians 2:3)
>
> When will God bring this war to an end? It is when the western confederacy, threatened by the kings of the east, comes back to the Holy Land to fight the eastern confederacy (Daniel 11:44). Instead of fighting each other, however, their animosity is

turned against the Lord from heaven who slays his enemies (Revelation 19:21). (James, *Arabs*, pp. 89-90)

Do the Ancient Prophecies Fit the Modern Facts?

The Possibility of Worldwide Destruction

In his address to the nation on March 6, 1991, President George Bush commented that "even a New World Order cannot guarantee a world of perpetual peace." Not one person living can deny that the massive proliferation of nuclear weapons in the modern era makes a worldwide Armageddon possible for the first time in human history. In fact, the Scripture quoted above in Zechariah 14:12 sounds surprisingly like the results of nuclear warfare: "This is the plague with which the Lord will strike all the nations that fought against Jerusalem: Their flesh will rot while they are still standing on their feet, their eyes will rot in their sockets, and their tongues will rot in their mouths" (Zechariah 14:12).

Nobel laureate Alfred Kastler has commented, "There is no need to be a great scholar or great prophet to see that the human race is rushing toward its suicide" (p. 20). Other authorities, such as former editor-in-chief of *The Bulletin of the Atomic Scientists*, Bernard T. Feld, have said that we are entering the most dangerous period in the entire history of the world. Feld himself gives the chances as being greater than 50/50 for a nuclear war to take place in the remaining years of this century (p. 8).

William Epstein, special consultant on disarmament to the U.N. has worked on arms control problems for a quarter century. In his book *The Last Chance: Nuclear Proliferation And Arms Control*, he sees the possibility of a nuclear holocaust as having risen to a near certainty (p. 142).

Among the many conclusions of five experts at a Harvard-MIT Arms Control Seminar were:

1. that nuclear war in some form was likely before the end of the century;
2. that if nations of the world are to survive, they may have to surrender their national sovereignty. ("Nuclear War by 1999?" pp. 32-43).

Arms races have almost universally ended in war (a chance of 99.1 percent) and 100 percent of those that did not end in war resulted in economic collapse for the countries involved. Analysis from the *Stockton Herald* of California discusses a computer survey that revealed that since 3600 B.C. the world has known only 292 years of peace. In that period of 55 centuries, there have been 14,530 wars killing over 3.6 billion people. Further, since 650 B.C., there have been 1,656 arms races, and all except 16 ended in war; the other 16 ended in the economic collapse of the countries involved.

According to Paul Doty, Mallinckrodt Professor of Biochemistry at Harvard University, contributor to the *Bulletin of the Atomic Scientists* and member of a Harvard-MIT Arms Control Seminar, some 30 million people died in wars between 1915 and 1945, not including Civil War deaths ("Nuclear War by 1999?" pp. 34). Frank Barnaby, director of the prestigious Stockholm International Peace Research Institute, observes that between 1945 and 1975 there have been 119 activities that could be defined as war, either civil or international. Total duration of those conflicts added together would exceed 350 years involving the territory of 69 countries and the armed forces of 81 states, including the deaths of several tens of millions of people. Indeed, he tells us that since September, 1945, there has not been a single day in which there has not been one or more wars being fought somewhere in the world, with about twelve wars being waged on an "average" day (p. 25).

As of this writing, over a dozen large and small wars are being fought around the world in Albania, Laos, Liberia, Rwanda, and other countries. In the last few years there have been thirty-seven major wars (each having more than 1,000 casualties) and seventy-five minor wars. More than 1 million died in the

Afghanistan war and up to 100 million have died in wars in the last ninety years alone.

In conclusion, history has shown that man's nature has been to go to war and that today war is still taking place in many parts of the world. Finally, the Middle East continues to face many of the same age old hatreds and problems. The only difference is that today these nations are beginning to arm with weapons of mass destruction. Sadly, the Bible predicts there will be an Armageddon.

The Strategic Military Importance Both in History and Today of the Plain of Esdraelon Near Megiddo

The general area that the Bible describes as the site of the battle of Armageddon is of known strategic military importance. Many wars have been fought in this region in the attempt to control the crossroads of the Middle East. Many times the authors have stood above this plain and taken in the vast panorama before them. It is not at all inconceivable that the major armies of the world could converge here for Armageddon.

The *Encyclopedia Britannica* makes the following comments about Armageddon:

> According to the New Testament, the place where the kings of the Earth under demonic leadership will wage war on the forces of God at the end of world history. The Palestinian city of Megiddo was probably used as a symbol [for Armageddon] because the strategic location of nearby mountains made them a famous battlefield in Palestinian history. By controlling a pass that cuts through the Mount Carmel ridge from the coastal plain of Sharon into Esdraelon, the mountains commanded the road leading from Egypt and the coastal plane of Palestine to Galilee, Syria, and Mesopotamia." (p. 522)

Significantly, the plain of Megiddo can be entered from all the points of the compass. Historically, battles have occurred here between Romans and Arabs, Crusaders and Turks, Babylonians and Greeks, Egyptians and Assyrians, and other peoples. This is why Napoleon referred to it as "the world's greatest natural battlefield" due to the ideal terrain for armies to maneuver (Tan, *Signs*, p. 164). Herman A. Hoyt has described the boundaries of Armageddon as follows:

> The battlefield stretches from Megiddo on the north (Zech. 12:11; Rev. 16:16) to Edom on the south (Isa. 34:5-6; 63:1), a distance of approximately 200 miles.
>
> It reaches from the Mediterranean Sea on the west to the hills of Moab on the east, a distance of almost 100 miles. It includes the valleys of Jehoshaphat (Joel 3:2) and the plains of Esdraelon. The center of the entire area is the city of Jerusalem (Zech. 14:1-2). The kings with their armies come from the north and the south, and from the east and from the west. (Tan, *Signs*, p. 65)

In conclusion, given the history of this location and its strategic military importance, plus the increasing importance of the general area of the Middle East today, it is more and more plausible that Armageddon could be fought here. In the lifetime of the reader of this book, Armageddon could actually happen.

China's Potential Army of 200 Million Men

No one can deny that it is now possible for the nations of the Orient to muster an army of 200 million soldiers. A number of years ago, a television documentary on Red China, entitled "The Voice of the Dragon," cited the Chinese boasting that they alone could field a "people's army" of 200 million men. We have noted in this chapter that in Revelation 9:13-16 the Bible describes a massive army from the east, 200 million strong, which marches to Israel for the battle of Armageddon. The Bible says that these 200 million soldiers will march to Israel down the dried up Euphrates river. The Euphrates is the longest river in western Asia, about 1700 miles in length. It marks the boundary between Israel and her historic enemies, Assyria and Babylon (Revelation 9:13-16; 16:12-16).

In conclusion, the possible use of weapons of mass destruction along with the historic military importance of the valley of Megiddo and the amazing fact that an army of 200 million men can now be marshalled from the East all prove that the conditions of our day could bring about the battle of Armageddon. Up to this point, we have examined some of the amazing biblical predictions concerning the last days—the restoration and importance of Israel, the dramatic rapture, a united world confederacy ruled by a dictator, the Antichrist, a coming attack on Israel from the north, and a Great Tribulation period leading to the final battle of the world—Armageddon (LaSore, p. 45). But it is the next biblical prediction, the return of Jesus Christ, that is the most important prophecy of all; it will literally change the world—forever.

21

The Powerful Return of Jesus Christ To Earth

Do we not all spend the greater part of our lives under the shadow of an event that has not yet come to pass?

Maurice Maeterlinch

What Are the Ancient Biblical Prophecies?

Zechariah 14:2*a*, 3-4, 5-11 (500 B.C.):

> I will gather all the nations to Jerusalem to fight against it. . . . Then the Lord will go out and fight against those nations, as he fights in the day of battle. On that day his feet will stand on the Mount of Olives, east of Jerusalem, and the Mount of Olives will be split in two from east to west, forming a great valley. . . . Then the Lord my God will come, and all the holy ones with him. On that day there will be no light, no cold or frost. It will be a unique day, without daytime or nighttime—a day known to the Lord. . . . The Lord will be king over the whole earth. . . . Jerusalem will be raised up. . . . Never again will it be destroyed. (See also Zechariah 12:10.)

Daniel 2:44; 7:13-14 (530 B.C.):

> In the time of those kings, the God of heaven will set up a kingdom that will never be destroyed. . . . It will crush all those kingdoms and bring them to an end, but it will itself endure forever. . . . In my vision at night I [Daniel] looked, and there before me was one like a son of man, coming with the clouds of heaven. He approached the Ancient of Days and was led into his presence. He was given authority, glory and sovereign power; all peoples, nations and men of every language worshiped him. His dominion is an everlasting dominion that will not pass away, and His kingdom is one that will never be destroyed.

Matthew 24:14, 27, 30 (A.D. 50-70):

> [Jesus said,] And this gospel of the kingdom will be preached in the whole world as a testimony to all nations, and then the end will come. . . . For as lightning that comes from the east is visible even in the west, so will be the coming of the Son of Man. . . . At that time, the sign of the Son of Man will appear in the sky, and all the nations of the earth will mourn. They will see the Son of Man coming on the clouds in the sky, with power and great glory.

Revelation 20:1-2:

> And I saw an angel coming down out of heaven, having the key to the Abyss and holding in his hand a great chain. He seized the dragon, that ancient serpent, who is the devil, or Satan, and bound him for a thousand years.

If there is one fact that cannot be denied in the Bible, it is that Jesus Christ will personally return to this earth. The ancient prophets predicted it, Jesus Himself predicted it on repeated occasions, and the apostles predicted it (see Pache; 2 Peter 3:10-13; 2 Thessalonians 1:6-10; Jude 14-15).

The second coming of Christ is not an obscure biblical doctrine. The Bible speaks of the second coming of our Lord 1,845 times. In the New Testament it is dealt with 318 different times. Twenty-three of the twenty-seven books of the New Testament deal with the topic of the second coming. That means that every twenty-fifth verse of the New Testament has to do with the return of Jesus Christ.

For example, in Revelation 1:7 we are told "Look, he is coming with the clouds and every eye will see him." In Acts 1:11, the angels asked, "Men of Galilee, . . . why do you stand here looking into the sky? This same Jesus, who has been taken up from you into heaven, will come back in the same way you have seen him go into heaven." In 1 Corinthians 11:26, Paul reminds us, "For whenever you eat this bread and drink this cup, you proclaim the Lord's death until he comes." The apostle John in 1 John 3:2 states, "Dear friends, now we are children of God, and what we will be has not yet been made known. But we know that when he appears, we shall be like him, for we shall see him as he is."

No Christian need lack faith or assurance that Jesus is coming again. Jesus Himself calmed our doubts when He said in John 14:1-2, "Do not let your hearts be troubled. Trust in God; trust also in me. In My father's house are many rooms; if it were not so, I would have told you. I am going there to prepare a place for you. And if I go and prepare a place for you, I will come back and take you to be with me that you also may be where I am."

The Bible says that Jesus Christ Himself will return and put an end to the battle of Armageddon. From that moment on, the world will never be the same. The Bible describes this as the beginning of the millennial reign of Jesus Christ, a period of one thousand years of unparalleled prosperity, peace, and security. Revelation 20 clearly states that the devil himself will be bound and will not be permitted to deceive the nations any longer. "He seized the dragon, that ancient serpent, who is the devil, or Satan, and bound him for a thousand years. He threw him into the Abyss, and locked and sealed it over him, to keep him from deceiving the nations any more until the thousand years were ended" (Revelation 20:2-3).

Many passages in the Old Testament describe the messianic age, where Christ rules the world. One of the best known is Isaiah 11:6-9:

> The wolf will live with the lamb, the leopard will lie down with the goat, the calf and the lion and the yearling together; and a little child will lead them. The cow will feed with the bear, their young will lie down together, and the lion will eat straw like the ox. The infant will play near the hole of the cobra, and the young child will put his hand into the viper's nest. They will neither harm nor destroy on all my holy mountain, for the earth will be full of the knowledge of the Lord as the waters cover the sea.

The conditions of this period are reflected in the fact that even small children will not be harmed when they play with formerly ferocious or deadly animals. Isaiah the prophet described these days: "Never again will there be in it an infant who lives but a few days, or an old man who does not live out his years; he who dies at a hundred will be thought a mere youth; he who fails to reach a hundred will be considered accursed" (Isaiah 65:20).

At the end of the Millennium, the devil "must be set free for a short time" (Revelation 20:3). For one last time he will deceive the nations. But the devil and, unbelievably, those who follow him will be supernaturally destroyed by God (Revelation 20:7). It is at this point that the Bible describes an entirely new and eternal order that will never pass away:

> Then I saw a new heaven and a new earth, for the first heaven and the first earth had passed away, and there was no longer any sea. I saw the Holy City, the new Jerusalem, coming down out of heaven from God, prepared as a bride beautifully dressed for her husband. And I heard a loud voice from the throne saying, "Now the dwelling of God is with men, and he will live with them. They will be his people, and God himself will be with them and will be their God. He will wipe every tear from their eyes. There will be no more death or mourning or crying or pain, for the old order of things has passed away."

He who was seated on the throne said, "I am making everything new!" Then he said, "Write this down, for these words are trustworthy and true."

He said to me: "It is done. I am the Alpha and the Omega, the Beginning and the End. To him who is thirsty I will give to drink without cost from the spring of the water of life. He who overcomes will inherit all this, and I will be his God and he will be my son." (Revelation 21:1-7)

As Jesus said, *anyone who wishes* may partake of these future events and inherit an eternal life of unimagined joy and unparalleled blessing—simply by believing on Him for forgiveness of sins (John 3:16).

Do the Ancient Prophecies Fit the Modern Facts?

If we carefully examine the current military, economic, and geopolitical situation of the world, and then carefully examine what the Bible predicts will occur prior to the second coming of Christ, one must acknowledge that many current day events are beginning to parallel what the Bible says must take place. What conclusions should these startling predictions lead a thoughtful person to consider? To this important topic we now turn.

22
Almighty God's Promise to Men

We know what we are, but know not what we may be.
Hamlet

What does all this mean? It means it is now possible that we are really in the last days of the world. Biblical prophecy is too detailed and too precise to ignore. If we are in or approaching the period preceding the coming of Christ, then this has major implications for the life of every person.

If we are approaching the events that mark the Great Tribulation period and the return of Christ, then no one anywhere can be unconcerned. Christians need to be engaged in the task of evangelism. The reason should be obvious: No one can logically deny the biblical record of predicting the future—and that record seems to speak directly to our particular historical period.

Perhaps you, the reader, have never thought of receiving Christ as your personal Savior. The Bible tells us that "now is the day of salvation" (2 Corinthians 6:2), because no man or woman has a guarantee of living till tomorrow.

As you consider biblical prophecy and the current conditions of the world, consider your own future. If God offers everyone a free gift of salvation so that they will have the possibility of living forever in heaven, isn't this gift something to be desired? Is it something that you desire right now?

The Bible admonishes each of us, "See to it that you do not refuse him [God] who speaks. If they did not escape when they refused him who warned them on earth, how much less will we, if we turn away from him who warns us from heaven?" (Hebrews 12:25) The writer of Hebrews warned the people in his own day: "We must pay more careful attention, therefore, to what we have heard, so that we do not drift away. For if the message spoken by angels was binding, and every violation and disobedience received its just punishment, how shall we escape if we ignore such a great salvation?" (Hebrews 2:1-3a).

In addition to warning people to pay attention to what God has spoken, he also warns of not believing in God's promises: "See to it, brothers, that none of you has a sinful, unbelieving heart that turns away from the living God. But encourage one another daily, as long as it is called Today, so that none of you may be hardened by sin's deceitfulness" (Hebrews 3:12-13). What does God advise you to do in order to inherit eternal life?

1. Acknowledge your condition before God and admit your need. "For the wages of sin is death, but the gift of God is eternal life in Christ Jesus our Lord" (Romans 6:23).

2. Jesus provided the free gift of salvation by dying on the cross. "For Christ died for sins once for all, the righteous for the unrighteous, to bring you to God" (1 Peter 3:18). "But God demonstrates his own love for us in this: While we were still sinners, Christ died for us" (Romans 5:8).

3. You must personally receive Christ as your Savior. "Yet to all who received him, to those who believed in his name, he gave the right to become children of God" (John 1:12). "For, 'Everyone who calls on the name of the Lord will be saved'" (Romans 10:13). "Here I am! I stand at the door and knock. If anyone hears my voice

and opens the door, I will come in and eat with him, and he with me" (Revelation 3:20).

How can you be certain of gaining heaven? If you wish to receive Christ as your personal Savior, we would suggest you pray the following prayer:

Dear God: It is my desire to receive Christ as my personal Savior. I confess that I am a sinner and acknowledge that Jesus Christ died on the cross for my sins. I now receive you as my Savior, recognizing that you died on the cross in payment for my sins. I ask you to come into my life and to make my life pleasing to you. In Jesus' name. Amen.

If you have just prayed that prayer, God promises that you are now a Christian. God has now forgiven all your sins—past, present, and future. A place in heaven is reserved for you, kept safe from all possibility of loss because it "can never perish" (1 Peter 1:3-5). God has now made you alive spiritually and come to dwell within you. As a new Christian, it is your responsibility to know God better by prayer, reading His Word in the Bible, and fellowshipping with other Christians at a church that respects Christ and His Word.

We also suggest that you study basic biblical teaching as found in such books as J. I. Packer, *God's Words*, and Francis Schaeffer, *True Spirituality*. The Bible encourages every believer to "grow in the grace and knowledge of our Lord and Savior Jesus Christ" (2 Peter 3:18). It is our prayer that you will do this and thereby honor the God who has not only given you life, but died so that you now have eternal life (John 3:16).

What Jesus said to the Christian is also applicable to all people: "So you also must be ready, because the Son of Man will come at an hour when you do not expect him" (Matthew 24:44).

BIBLIOGRAPHY

Adler, Mortimer J. *How To Think About God.* New York: Bantam, 1988.

Alexander, Ralph. "Ezekiel." In vol. 6 of the *Expositors' Bible Commentary*, edited by Frank E. Gaebelin. Grand Rapids: Zondervan, 1986.

Alford, Henry. *Alford's Greek Testament.* Grand Rapids: Guardian, 1976.

Anderson, Sir Robert. *The Coming Prince.* 10th ed. Reprint. Grand Rapids: Kregel, 1954.

Ankerberg, John, and John Weldon. *Can You Trust Your Doctor? The Complete Guide to New Age Medicine and Its Threat to Your Family.* Brentwood, Tenn.: Wolgemuth & Hyatt, 1991.

_____ . *The Case for Jesus the Messiah: Incredible Prophecies That Prove God Exists.* Chattanooga, Tenn.: Ankerberg Theological Research Institute, 1988.

_____ . *The Facts on Islam.* Eugene, Oreg.: Harvest House, 1991.

_____ . *The Facts on Astrology.* Eugene, Oreg.: Harvest House, 1989.

_____ . *The Facts on the Mormon Church.* Eugene, Oreg.: Harvest House, 1991.

_____ . *The Facts on the New Age Movement.* Eugene, Oreg.: Harvest House, 1988.

_____ . *The Facts on the Occult.* Eugene, Oreg.: Harvest House, 1991.

_____ . *The Facts on Spirit Guides.* Eugene, Oreg.: Harvest House, 1991.

_____ . *Cultwatch.* Eugene, Oreg.: Harvest House, 1991.

_____ . *Astrology.* Eugene, Oreg.: Harvest House, 1989.

_____ . *Do the Resurrection Accounts Conflict? and What Proof Is There That Jesus Christ Rose from the Dead?* Chattanooga, Tenn.: Ankerberg Theological Research Institute, 1990.

Arberry, A. J. *The Koran Interpreted.* New York: MacMillan, 1976.

Archer, Gleason. "Daniel." In vol. 7 of the *Expositors' Bible Commentary*, edited by Frank E. Gaebelein. Grand Rapids: Zondervan, 1985.

_____ . *Encyclopedia of Bible Difficulties.* Grand Rapids: Zondervan, 1982.

_____ . *A Survey Of Old Testament Introduction.* Chicago: Moody, 1974.

Barnaby, Frank. "World Armament and Disarmament—A Report to the Stockton International Peace Research Institute on the Growing Arsenals of War." *Bulletin of the Atomic Scientists* (June 1976).

Bass, Clarence G. *Backgrounds to Dispensationalism*. Grand Rapids: Baker, 1981.

Becher, Willis Judson. *The Prophets and the Promise*. New York: Thomas Crowell, 1905.

Ben-Sasson, H. H. *A History of the Jewish People*. Cambridge, Mass.: Harvard U., 1976.

Bjornstad, James. *20th Century Prophecy: Jeane Dixon–Edgar Cayce*. Minneapolis: Bethany Fellowship, 1969.

Blanchard, John, comp. *More Gathered Gold*. Hertfordshire, Eng.: Evangelical Press, 1986.

Boutflower, Charles. *In and Around the Book of Daniel*. Reprint. Grand Rapids: Kregel, 1977.

Bradbury, John W. *The Sure Word of Prophecy*. New York: Ravel, 1943.

Breese, Dave. *Europe and the Prince That Shall Come*. Hillsboro, Kan.: Christian Destiny, n.d.

Brown, Colin. *Miracles and the Critical Mind*. Grand Rapids: Eerdmans, 1984.

Cetron, Marvin. *Encounters with the Future*. New York: McGraw Hill, 1982.

Clarke, Arthur C. *July 20, 2019: Life in the 21st Century*. New York: MacMillan, 1986.

Clouse, Robert G. *The Meaning of the Millennium: Four Views*. Downers Grove, Ill.: InterVarsity, 1979.

Cox, William E. *Amillennialism Today*. Nutley, N.J.: Presby. & Ref., 1977.

Cross, F. L., ed. *The Oxford Dictionary of the Christian Church*. Oxford: Oxford U., 1985.

Custance, Arthur. "Some Striking Fulfillments of Prophecy." In *Hidden Things of God's Revelation*. Grand Rapids: Zondervan, 1977.

Dawood, N. J. *The Koran*. Baltimore: Penguin, 1972.

Edersheim, Alfred. *Prophecy and History in Relation to the Messiah*. Grand Rapids: Baker, 1955.

Edghill, E. A. *An Enquiry into the Evidential Value of Prophecy*. London: MacMillan, 1906.

Fairbairn, Patrick. *The Interpretation of Prophecy*. Reprint. London: Banner of Truth Trust, 1964.

Feinberg, Charles Lee, ed. *Prophecies in the Seventies*. Chicago: Moody, 1971.

_____ . *The Prophecy of Ezekiel*. Chicago: Moody, 1969.

Feld, Bernard T. "The Charade of Peacemeal Arms Limitations." *Bulletin of the Atomic Scientists* (January 1975).

Freeman, Hobart. *An Introduction to the Old Testament Prophets.* Chicago: Moody, 1968.

Fruchtenbaum, Arnold G. *The Footsteps of the Messiah: A Study of the Sequence of Prophetic Events.* San Antonio, Tex.: Ariel, 1982.

Geisler, Norman. *Christ: The Theme of the Bible.* Chicago: Moody, 1969.

———. *A Popular Survey of the Old Testament.* Grand Rapids: Baker, 1978.

Glueck, Nelson. *Rivers in the Desert.* New York: Farrar, Strauss & Cudahy, 1959.

Gillon, Philip. "The Core of the Problem." *The Jerusalem Post,* September 12, 1975.

Grant, George. *The Blood of the Moon: The Roots of the Middle East Crisis.* Brentwood, Tenn.: Wolgemuth & Hyatt, 1991.

Gurney, Robert J. M. et al. "Approaching Daniel: Three Studies." *Themelios* (January 1977).

Harrison, Everett F., ed. *Baker's Dictionary of Theology.* Grand Rapids: Baker, 1972.

Hengstenberg, E. W. *Christology of the Old Testament.* Reprint. Grand Rapids: Kregel, 1971.

Hilberg, Raul. *The Destruction of the European Jews.* New York: Harper Colophon, 1961.

Hoekema, Anthony. *The Bible and the Future.* Grand Rapids: Eerdmans, 1979.

Hunt, Dave. *CIB Bulletin* (April 1991).

———. *Global Peace and the Rise of Antichrist.* Eugene, Oreg.: Harvest House, 1990.

Ibraham, Ishak. *Black Gold and Holy War.* New York, Nelson, 1983.

Israel My Glory (October/November 1990).

James, Edgar C. *Arabs, Oil, and Armageddon.* Chicago: Moody, 1991.

———. "Prophecy and the Common Market." *Moody Monthly* (March 1974).

Johnson, Alan F. "Revelation." In vol. 12 of the *Expositors' Bible Commentary,* edited by Frank E. Gaebelein. Grand Rapids: Zondervan, 1979.

Kaiser, Walter C. "Legitimate Hermeneutics." In *Inerrancy,* edited by Norman L. Geisler. Grand Rapids: Zondervan, 1979.

Kastler, Alfred. "The Challenge of the Century." *Bulletin of the Atomic Scientists* (September 1977).

Keil, C. F., and F. Delitzsch. *Commentary on the Old Testament in Ten Volumes.* Grand Rapids: Eerdmans, 1978.

Kelly, J. N. D. *Early Christian Doctrines*. Rev. ed. New York: Harper & Row, 1978.

Kitchen, K. A. *Ancient Orient and the Old Testament*. Chicago: InterVarsity, 1973.

_____ . *Notes on Some Problems in the Book of Daniel*. London: Tyndale, 1965.

LaLonde, Peter. *The Omega Letter* (March 1991).

LaSore, William Sanford. *The Truth About Armageddon: What the Bible Says About the End Times*. Grand Rapids: Baker, 1972.

Lenski, R. C. H. *The Interpretation of St. Luke's Gospel*. Minneapolis: Augsburg, 1961.

Levitt, Zola. *Satan in the Sanctuary*. Chicago: Moody, 1973.

_____ . *Israel in Agony: The Beginning of the End?* Irvine, Calif.: Harvest House, 1975.

Lewis, C. D. "Modern Theology and Biblical Criticism." In *Christian Reflections*. Grand Rapids: Eerdmans, 1971.

Lewis, Charelton T., and Charles Short. *Latin Dictionary*. Oxford, Eng.: Oxford U., 1879.

Lewis, C. S. *Miracles*. London: Fontana, 1972.

Lindblom, J. *Prophecy in Ancient Israel*. Philadephia, Pa.: Fortress, 1976.

Lindsey, Hal. *The Late Great Planet Earth*. Grand Rapids: Zondervan, 1972.

_____ . *The Rapture*. New York: Bantam, 1984.

_____ . *The Road to Holocaust*. New York: Bantam, 1990.

Ludwigson, Raymond. *A Survey of Bible Prophecy*. Grand Rapids: Zondervan, 1973.

Machen, J. Gresham. *Christianity and Liberalism*. Grand Rapids: Eerdmans, 1972.

Maier, Gerhard. *The End of the Historical-Critical Method*. St. Louis, Mo.: Concordia, 1977.

McCall, Thomas, and Zola Levitt. *The Coming Russian Invasion of Israel*. Updated. Chicago: Moody, 1987.

McClain, Alva J. *Daniel's Prophecy of the 70 Weeks*. Grand Rapids: Zondervan, 1969.

_____ . *The Greatness of the Kingdom*. Grand Rapids: Zondervan, 1959.

McDowell, Josh. *Daniel in the Critics' Den: Historical Evidence for the Authenticity of the Book of Daniel*. San Bernardino, Calif.: Campus Crusade for Christ, 1973.

_____ . *Evidence That Demands a Verdict*. San Bernardino, Calif.: Campus Crusade for Christ, 1976.

_____ . *A Ready Defense*. San Bernardino, Calif.: Campus Crusade for Christ, 1988.

McKechnie, Jean L., editorial staff supervisor. *Webster's Twentieth Century Dictionary Unabridged*. 2d ed. New York: World Publishing, 1971.

Macrae, Norman. *The 2025 Report*. New York: MacMillan. 1984.

Montgomery, John W., ed. *Christianity for the Tough Minded*. Minneapolis: Bethany, 1973.

Morris, Henry. *Many Infallible Proofs*. San Diego, Calif.: Creation Life, 1974.

"Nuclear War By 1999? Five Experts Think It Likely." *Current* (January 1976).

Otis, George, Jr. "The Threat of a New Islamic Alliance." *Charisma* (April 1991)

Oxtoby, Gurdon. *Prediction and Fulfillment in the Bible*. Philadelphia: Westminister, 1966.

Pache, Rene. *The Return of Jesus Christ*. Chicago: Moody, 1955.

Payne, J. Barton. *Encyclopedia of Biblical Prophecy*. New York: Harper & Row, 1973.

Pentacost, J. Dwight. *Things to Come*. Findley, Ohio: Dunham, 1958.

Perspective (July/August 1976) book review.

Pink, Arthur W. *The Divine Inspiration of the Bible*. Grand Rapids: Baker, 1971.

Puharich, Andrija. *Uri*. New York: Bantam, 1975.

Ramm, Bernard M. *Protestant Christian Evidences*. Chicago: Moody, 1971.

Rodwell, J. M., trans. *The Koran*. Everyman's Library. New York: Dutton, 1977.

Ryrie, Charles. *The Basis of the Premillennial Faith*. Neptune, N.J.: Loizeaux, 1972.

Schaff, Philip. *The History of the Christian Church*. Ante-Nicene Christianity, vol. 2. Grand Rapids: Eerdmans, 1976.

Shorrosh, Anis. *Islam Revealed*. Nashville: Nelson, 1988.

Siegal, Bernie. *Love, Medicine and Miracles*. New York: Harper & Row, 1986.

Solzhenitsyn, Alexander. *Warning to the West*. New York: Farrar, Strauss and Giroux, 1977.

Stoner, Peter. *Science Speaks*. Chicago: Moody, 1975.

Strong, Augustus H. *Strong's Exhaustive Concordance*.

Tan, Paul Lee. *The Interpretation of Prophecy*. Winona Lake, Ind.: Assurance, 1978.

_____ . *Signs of the Times: Encyclopedia of 7700 Illustrations*. Rockville, Md.: Assurance, 1979.

Tenney, Merrill C. *Interpreting Revelation*. Grand Rapids: Eerdmans, 1971.

"Terror: A Fundamental Conflict" (A 3-part investigation of political violence). A & E Premiers, March 3, 1991. PBS.

180

Thiele, Edwin R. *A Chronology of the Hebrew Kings*. Grand Rapids: Zondervan, 1978.

Toffler, Alvin. *The Eco-Spasm Report*. New York: Bantam, 1975.

_____ . *The Third Wave*. New York: William Morrow, 1980.

Toynbee, Arnold J., and Daisaku Ikeda. *The Toynbee-Ikeda Dialogue: Man Himself Must Choose*. New York: Kodansha International, 1976.

Unger, Merrill. *Great Neglected Prophecies*. Chicago: Scripture Press, 1955.

Urquhart, John. *The Wonders of Prophecy*. 9th ed. Harrisburg, Pa.: Christian Publications, n.d.

Vonnegut, Kurt. *Time*. March 18, 1974.

Walvoord, John F. *Armageddon: Oil and the Middle East Crisis*. Rev. ed. Grand Rapids: Zondervan, 1990.

_____ . *Daniel: The Key to Prophetic Revelation*. Chicago: Moody, 1971.

_____ . *Israel and Prophecy*. Grand Rapids: Zondervan, 1962.

_____ . *The Millennial Kingdom*. Grand Rapids: Zondervan, 1972.

_____ . *The Nations in Prophecy*. London: Pickering & Engles, 1967.

_____ et al. *Prophecy Round Table*. Rev. ed. Dallas: Dallas Theological Seminary, 1982.

_____ . *The Rapture Question*. Grand Rapids: Zondervan, 1972.

_____ . *The Revelation of Jesus Christ*. Chicago: Moody, 1978.

Wert, Sherwood Eliot. *Living Quotations for Christians*. New York: Harper & Row, 1974.

White, John Wesley. *Re-Entry*. Grand Rapids: Zondervan, 1971.

Wilson, Clifford, and John Weldon. *1980's: Decade of Shock*. San Diego, Calif.: Master, 1980.

Wilson, Robert Dick. *A Scientific Investigation of the Old Testament*. Chicago: Moody, 1967.

_____ . *Studies in the Book of Daniel*. Reprint. Grand Rapids: Baker, 1979.

Woods, Leon J. *The Prophets of Israel*. Grand Rapids: Baker, 1979.

Wyngaarden, Martin J. *The Future of the Kingdom in Prophecy and Fulfillment*. Grand Rapids: Baker, 1955.